MUSICIANS INSTITUTE

PRIVATE LESSONS

I0801053

PROGRESSIVE BLUES GUITAR

Modern Techniques for the Electric Guitarist

by Nick Kellie

To access video visit:
www.halleonard.com/mylibrary

Enter Code
2376-4985-4828-9249

Cover photo of Nick Kellie © Nelson Onofre

ISBN 978-1-5400-9340-0

HAL•LEONARD®

Visit Hal Leonard Online at
www.halleonard.com

Contact us:
Hal Leonard
7777 West Bluemound Road
Milwaukee, WI 53213
Email: info@halleonard.com

In Europe, contact:
Hal Leonard Europe Limited
42 Wigmore Street
Marylebone, London, W1U 2RN
Email: info@halleonardeurope.com

In Australia, contact
Hal Leonard Australia Pty. Ltd.
4 Lentara Court
Cheltenham, Victoria, 3192 Australia
Email: info@halleonard.com.au

Contents

1 Blues Progressions

The majority of songs, with few exceptions, consist of chords progressing from one into the next. This is called a *chord progression*. One of the most basic of blues progressions is as follows:

Example 1

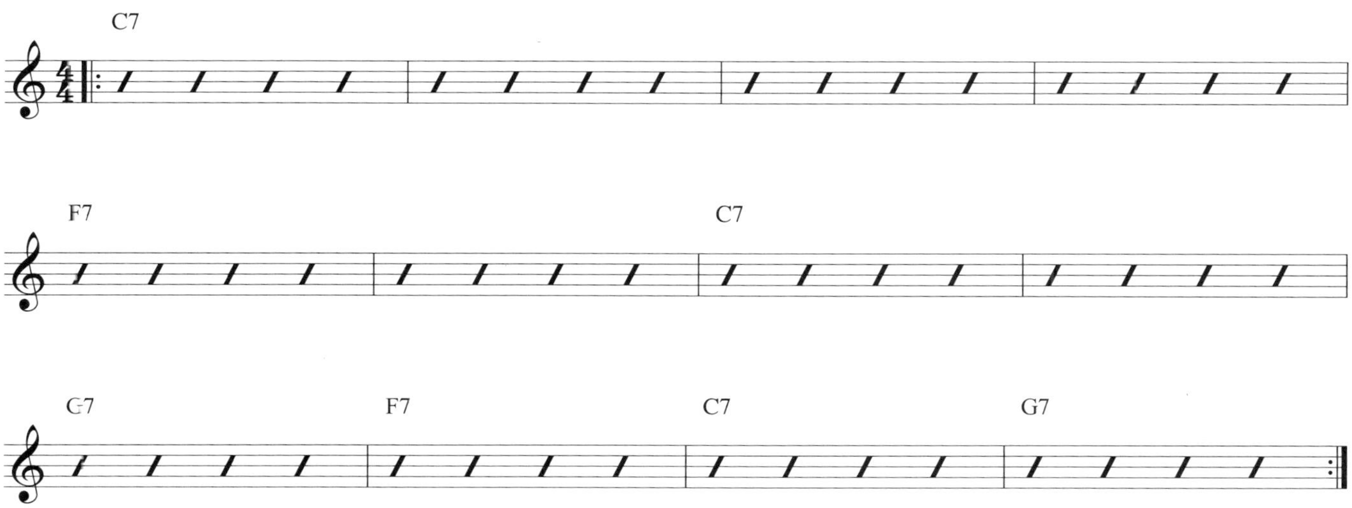

This chord progression is commonly known as the *12-bar blues*.

As well as expressing the chords using their letter names, we can also express them using Nashville numbers or Roman numerals. This is a convenient and neutral way of communicating a chord progression so a musician can put it into a key of their own choosing more easily. For example, each letter in the progression sits at a certain point within the key. In this case, the above progression originates from the key of C. In the key of C (consisting of the notes C, D, E, F, G, A, and B), the C note itself would be designated as the number "1" or Roman numeral "I," due to the fact that C is the first note within the key. F would be designated with the number "4" or Roman numeral "IV," since it is the fourth note in the key. Finally, the G note would be designated as the number "5" or Roman numeral "V," due to the fact that it is the fifth note within the key.

In order to communicate the chord type, we simply write a smaller signification after each note number. For example, C7 could be written as 1_7 or I7.

The advantage of this approach is that it facilitates easier transposition of a progression into any key. For example, if I wish to transpose the C7 and F7 chords by expressing them as 1_7 and 47, I can now easily move them into the key of G. 17 will now become G7 with 47 becoming C7 due to the new key having G as the first note and C as the fourth.

Here is the example from the previous page, expressed using Roman numerals:

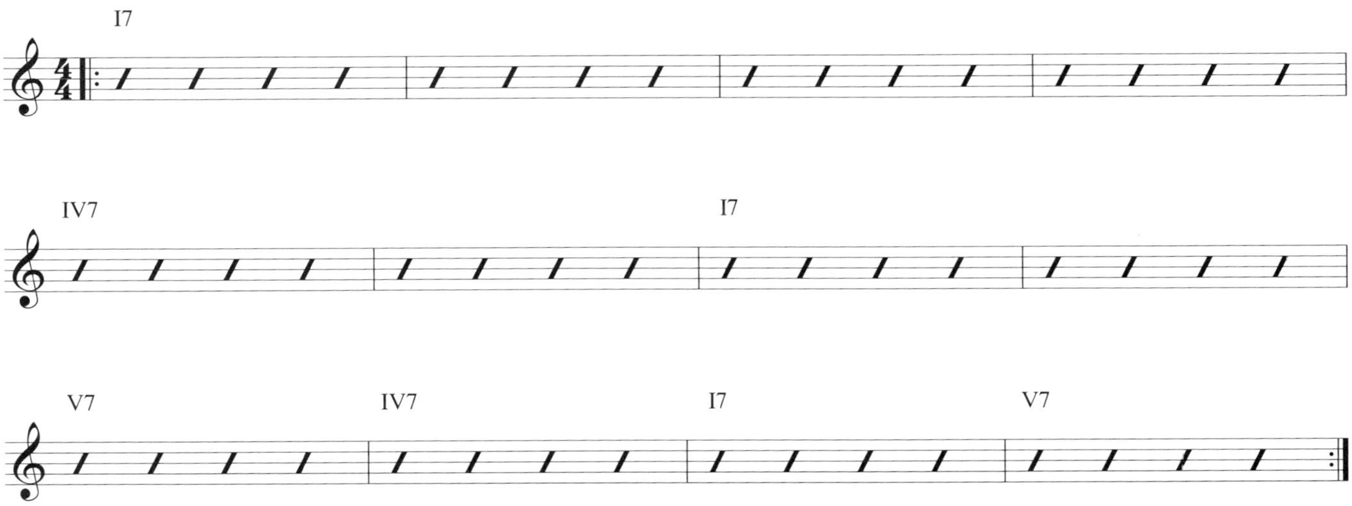

And here it is in a Nashville number chart:

4/4	1⁷	1⁷	1⁷	1⁷
	4⁷	4⁷	1⁷	1⁷
	5⁷	4⁷	1⁷	5⁷

I wanted to impart this theoretical information to you at the start of the book, as I always encourage all my students to transpose all these chord progressions into as many keys as possible. A good musician should be able to play in any key with ease. I believe that getting into the habit of seeing chord progressions as numerals will help you transpose quicker and, in turn, become a better musician. Let's take a look as some variations of the traditional 12-bar blues with a *quick change* to F7 in measure 2:

Example 2

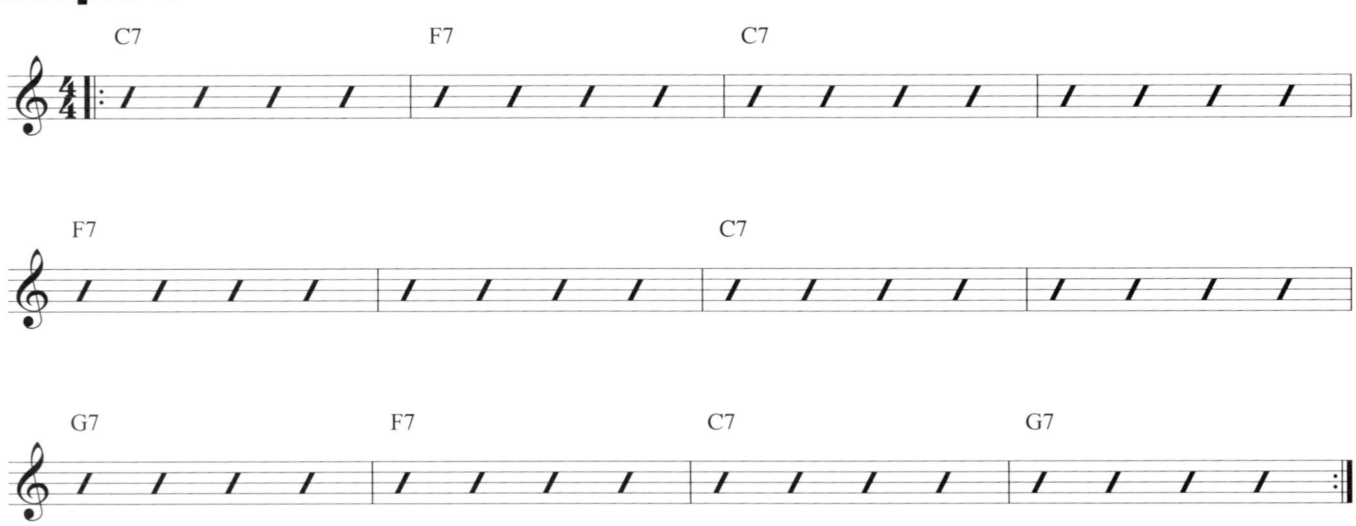

This is a very common, yet effective variation on the basic 12-bar blues seen in Example 1. The only difference is in measure 2, when we go to the 4 chord (F7) instead of staying on the 1 chord (C7). This creates less monotony and more interest and movement. Let's take a look at another simple addition that can spice things up even more:

Example 3

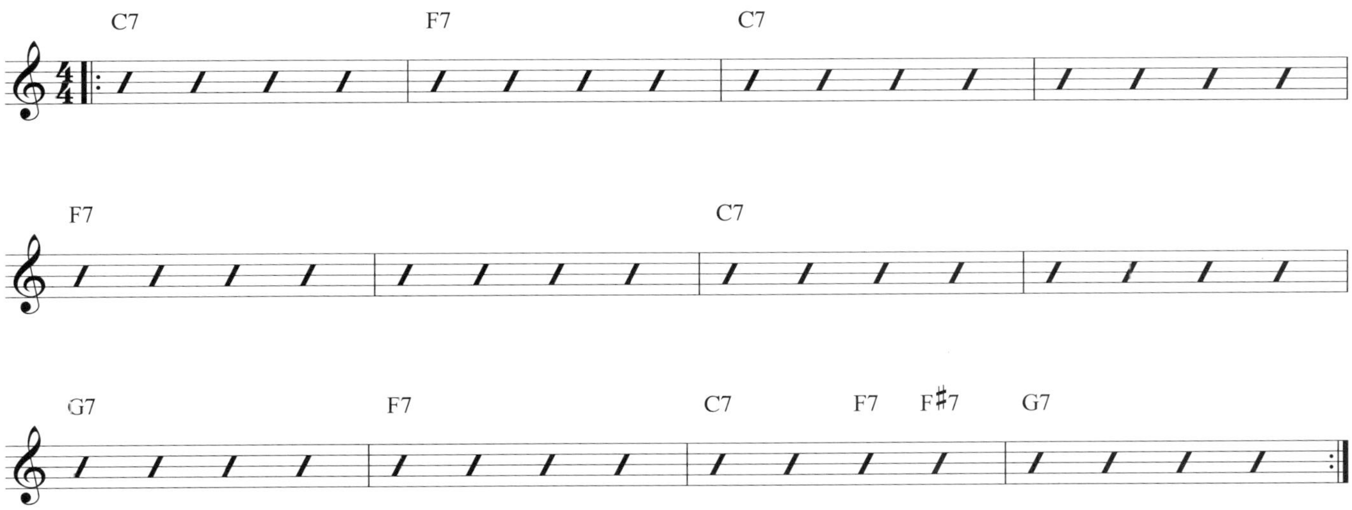

This example is identical to Example 3, except for the addition on measure 11 which introduces a chromatic walk-up into the 5 chord (G7). This creates a sense of leading the listener's ear into the chord.

Eventually, as we move into more complex variations, you will notice we get further and further away from our original 12-bar blues progression. Underneath all the fancy progressions, the original spirit and architecture remains.

Here is a more advanced variation where I have added a more intricate *turnaround* to the last two bars of the progression. The term turnaround refers to the fact that we are pulling the ear back to the beginning of the chord progression. Here is that example:

Example 4

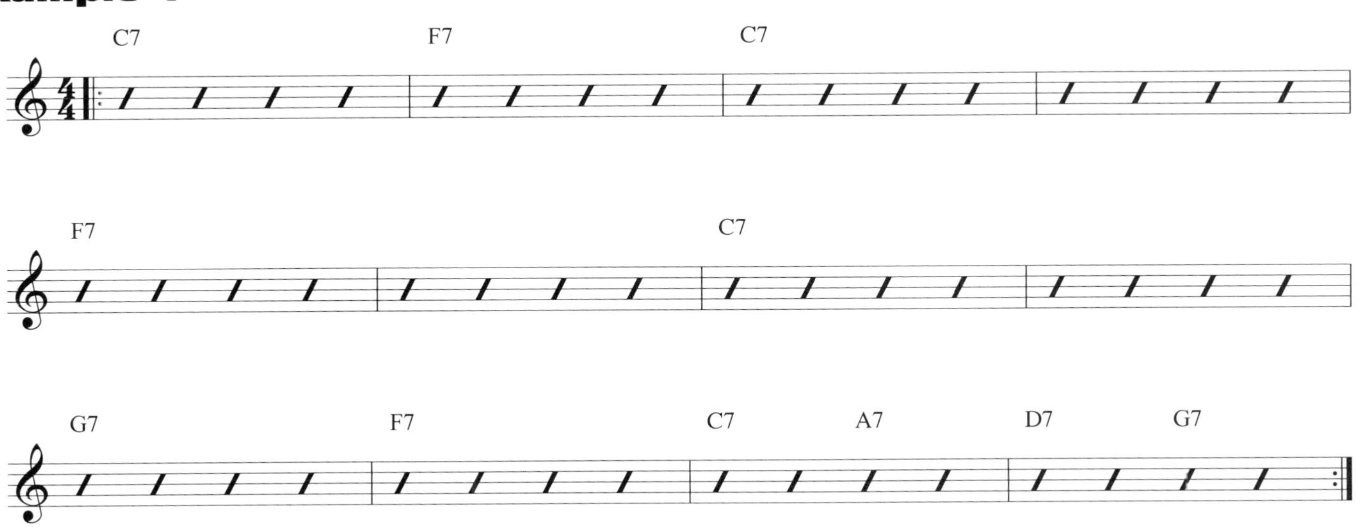

This is what is referred to as a *1–6–2–5 turnaround*. This incorporates the Nashville numbering system we talked about earlier: 1 being the C7, 6 is the A7, 2 is the D7 and 5 is the G7. These should be learned and applied in all keys. We can use this turnaround for the last two bars in any major blues.

Another cool thing we can do is approach each chord from a half step below or above. This is especially true when we go from the 1 chord to the 4 chord. It is common to approach the 4 chord from a half step above, a whole beat before it lands. Check out this example:

Example 5

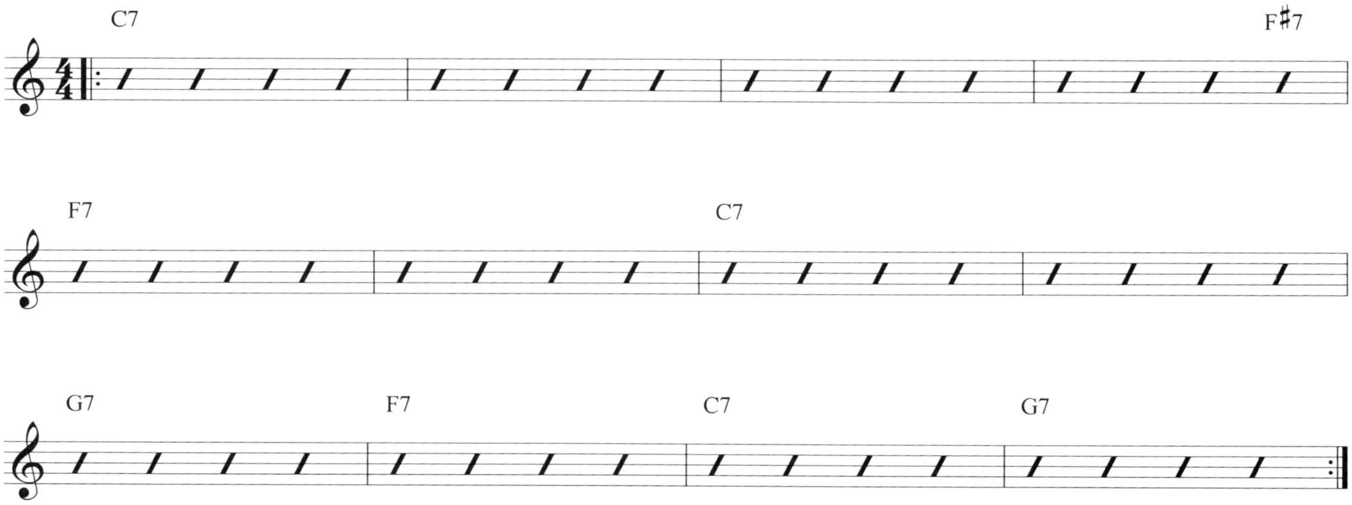

As you can see in the fourth beat of measure 4, we approach the 4 chord from a half step above by briefly playing F♯7. This leads the listener's ear into the next chord and gives a sense of movement.

Extending Chords

So far, we have been sticking exclusively to dominant 7th chords. It is also possible to extend any dominant chord by borrowing from its parent scale. For example, we generally associate each dominant 7th chord with the dominant (Mixolydian) scale. Essentially, this scale is just like a major scale but with the 7th degree lowered by a half step. Here is the major scale formula: 1–2–3–4–5–6–7. In C, this equates to the notes of C, D, E, F, G, A, and B. Compare this to C Mixolydian: 1–2–3–4–5–6–♭7. In C Mixolydian, this gives us the notes of C, D, E, F, G, A, and B♭. As you can see, the only difference is the 7th degree, which is lowered by a half step. In the key of C, this means the B note will become B♭.

In order to extend dominant 7th chords, we use the Mixolydian scale the majority of the time. Consider that chords are fundamentally built in 3rds. C7 has a formula of 1–3–5–♭7. This is the root of the C Mixolydian scale followed by every other note (3rds). If we continue beyond the ♭7, you'll see we have run out of notes in a one-octave scale. However, if we simply repeat the scale in the next octave, we get this:

1	2	3	4	5	6	♭7	8 (Octave)
	9	10	11	12	13	♭14	15 (Double Octave)

Therefore, if we keep adding 3rds on top of the C7, we can add notes such as 9, 11, and 13. A 9th interval is simply a 2nd in the next octave of the scale. If we add that ninth note on top of our C7, we end up with a C9 chord.

Here is the formula for C9: 1–3–5–♭7–9. In C, this equates to: C, E, G, B♭, and D.

These extended chords add so much color to the sound and give us a more sophisticated feel. Consider this as an alternative progression to the regular 12-bar blues:

Example 6

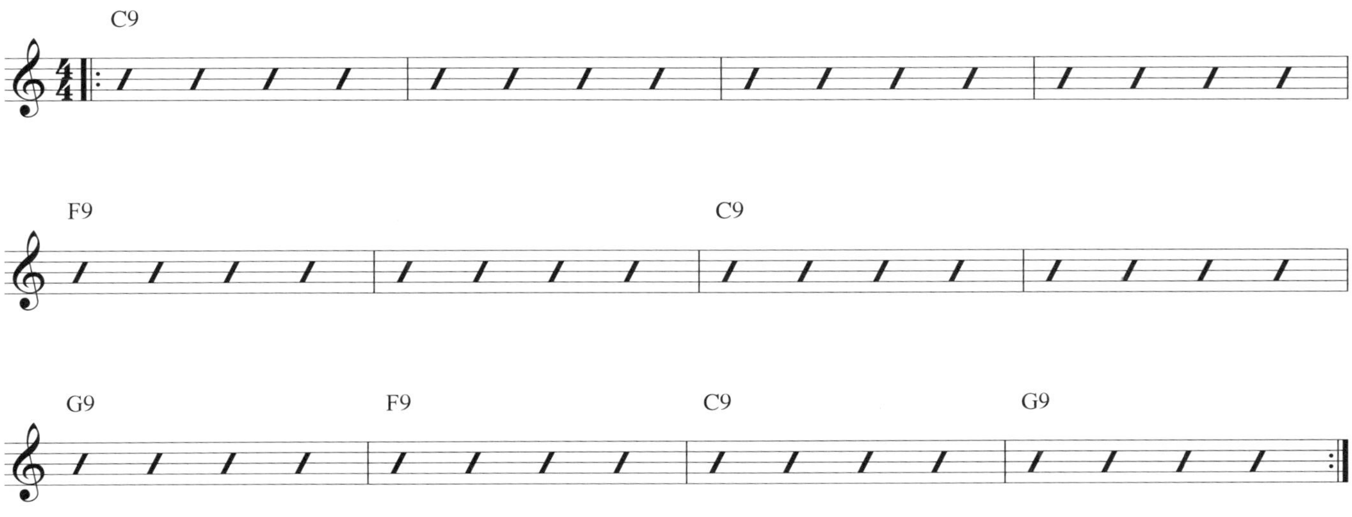

We don't necessarily have to use 9th chords for every single chord. We can mix and match and use to taste, but it is a great color to add to our musical palette as accompanists.

Here is an example that mixes 7th and 9th chords with the chromatic approach that we discussed earlier as we use the quick-change variation we discussed in Example 3.

Example 7

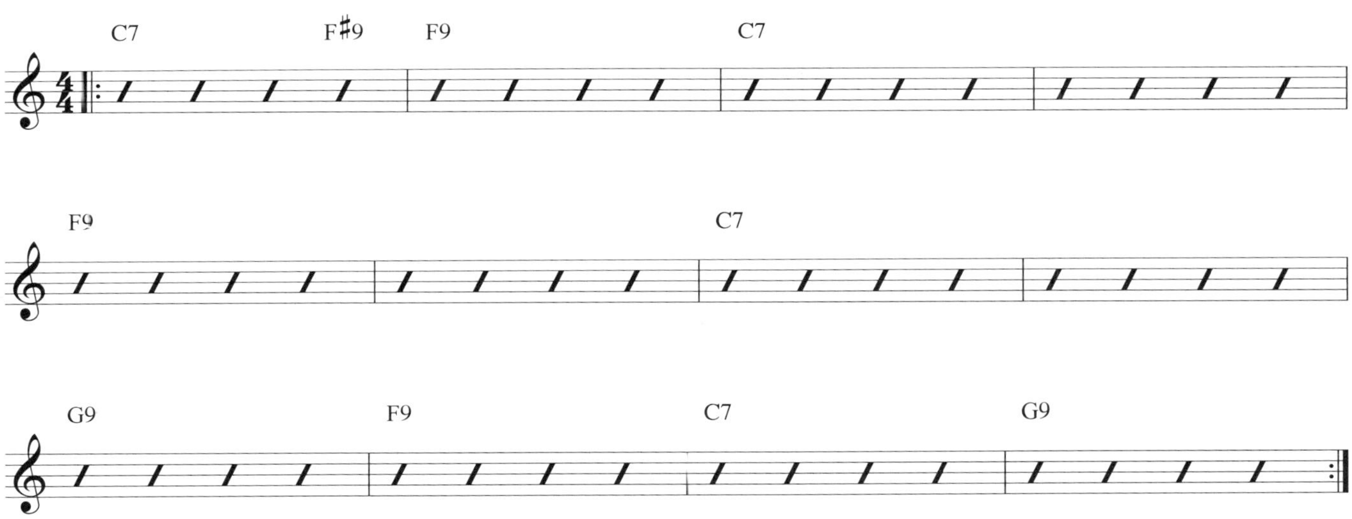

Altered Chords

Now I would like to talk about adding *altered chords* into the blues. An altered chord is where we add sharp or flat extensions onto the chord. Examples of altered chords would be G7♯9 or G7♭9. There are even more types of altered chords, but these two are the most common. Generally speaking, these are seen as a tense sound that needs to be resolved. Jimi Hendrix often broke that rule by using them in unresolved situations. For example, "Purple Haze" uses an E7♯9 as the 1 chord. In a blues context, we can use the 7♯9 chord on the 5 chord to resolve to the 1 chord, such as in measure 12 of our 12-bar blues.

Take a look at the example below:

Example 8

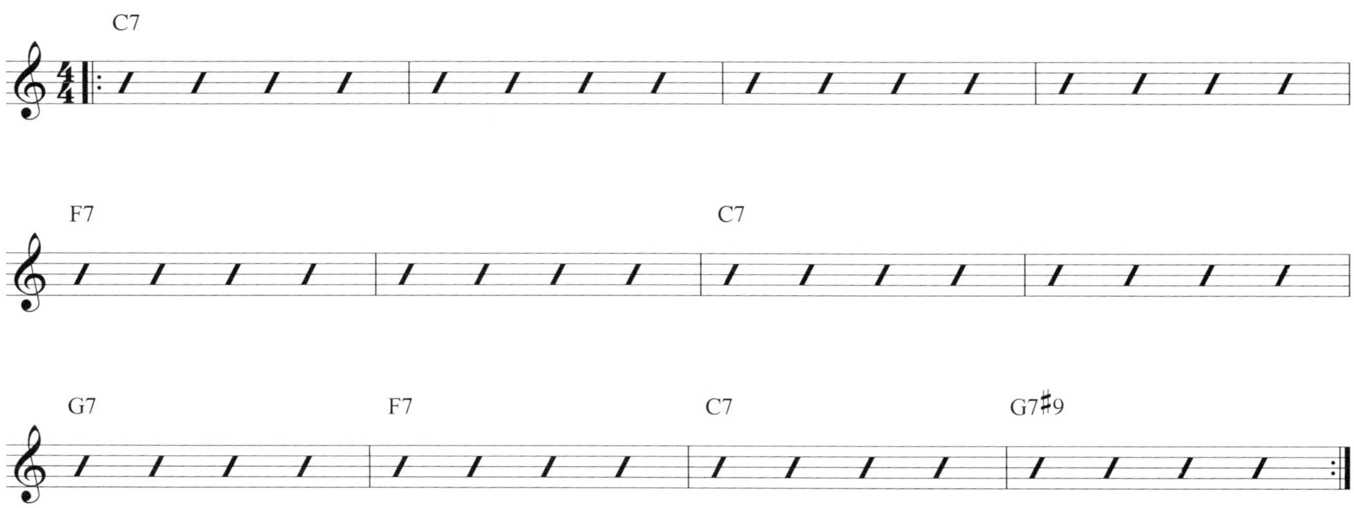

This gives us a feeling of tension in measure 12 which then leads to a greater sense of relief in measure 1.

Let's combine the approaches we have learned so far:

Example 9

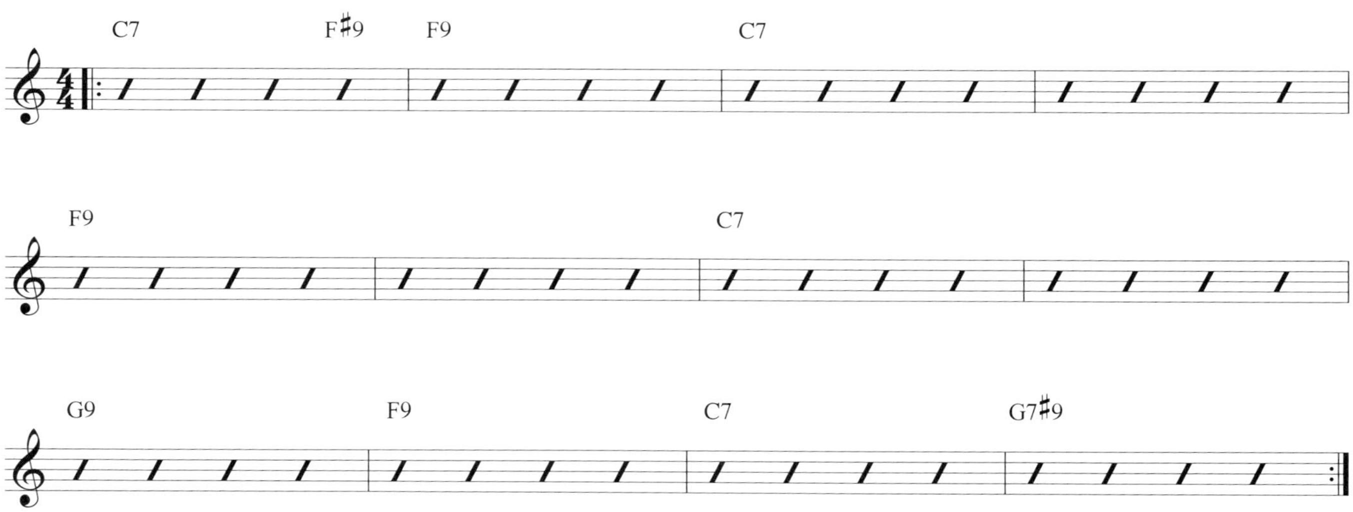

In this example, we see the use of a chromatic approach at the end of the first measure, as well as the use of 9th chords and then the altered ♯9 chord at the end of measure 12.

As we are moving through these examples, we can see that the blues is slowly transforming into something more harmonically complex but is still, at its heart, the blues.

Now I would like to add the altered V (5) chord into the 1–6–2–5 turnaround that we explored in Example 5:

Example 10

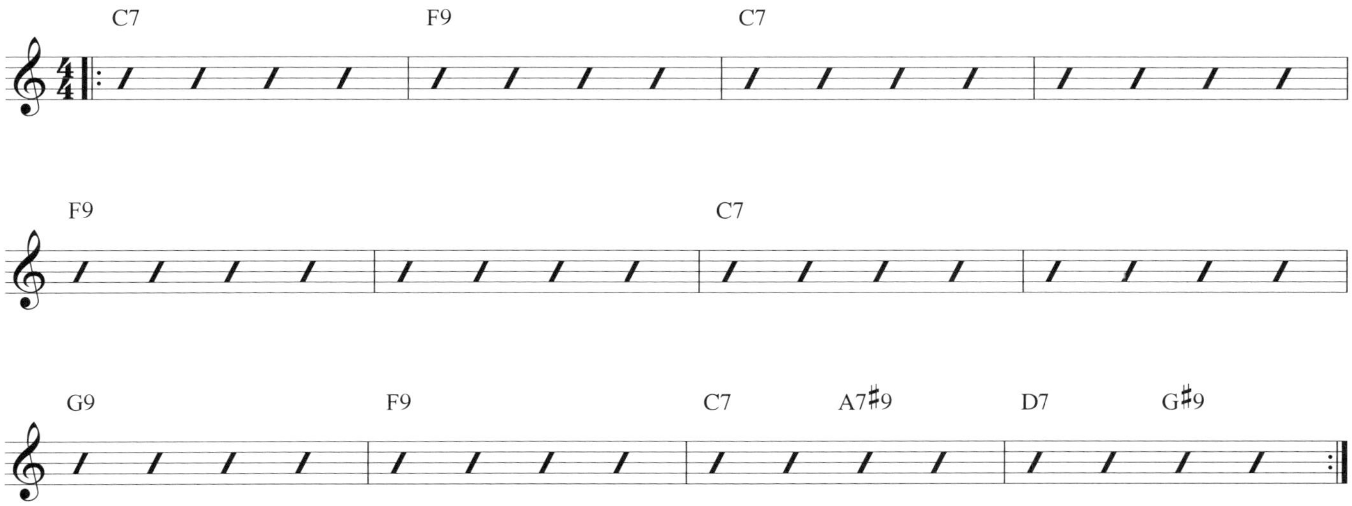

You will notice that I added the ♯9 onto the A7 and G7 chords, as they are essentially functioning as the V (5) chord to the chords that follow. A7 can be considered the V of D7 and G7 is the V of C7. This creates a colorful and interesting tension that works very well.

Now let's explore some new additions to the blues. Another common idea is to add the ii (2) chord into the mix. In the blues, we can think of the I chord (in this case C7) as being the V chord of the F7 chord. Whenever we move from the I (1) chord to the IV (4) chord, we can also see this in a reversed way and view the F7 chord as being I with C7 functioning as the V chord. Therefore, we can add in some interesting chord movements as follows:

Example 11

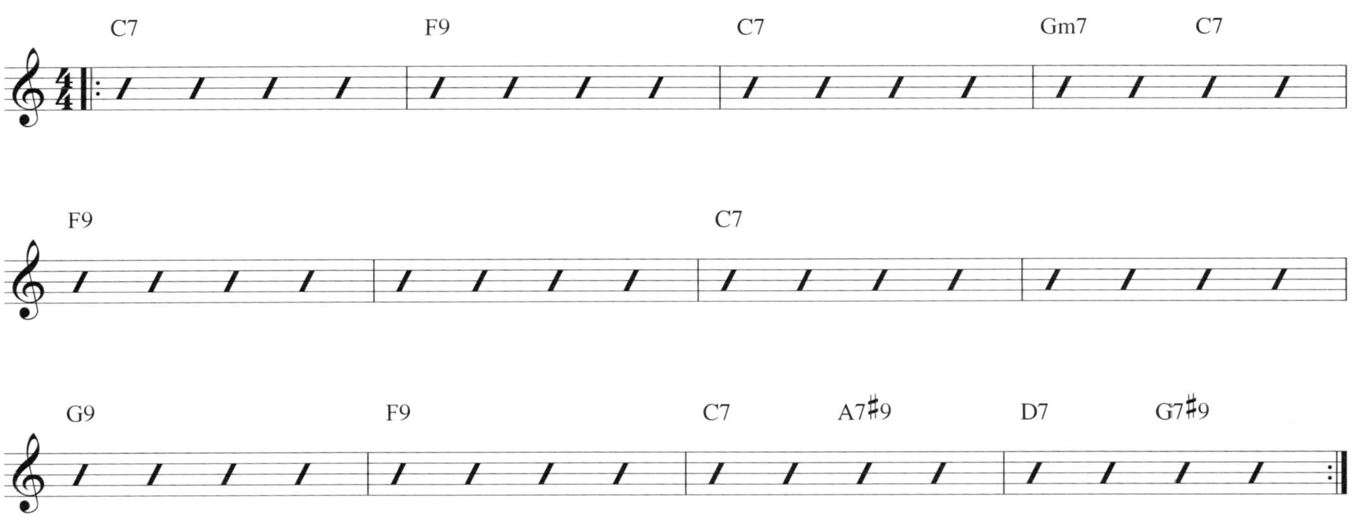

This example introduces a Gm7 as the ii chord to F9 in measure 4 in order to break the monotony of staying on the C7 chord for two whole bars in measures 3 and 4.

There are other devices we can use to break the monotony in other measures within the blues. Take a look at measures 5 and 6, or 7 and 8 in the blues. In both cases, we see two measures spent on 1 chord. We can break this monotony by using passing chords. A common example of that would be to use a diminished chord a half step up from the IV chord in measure 6:

Example 12

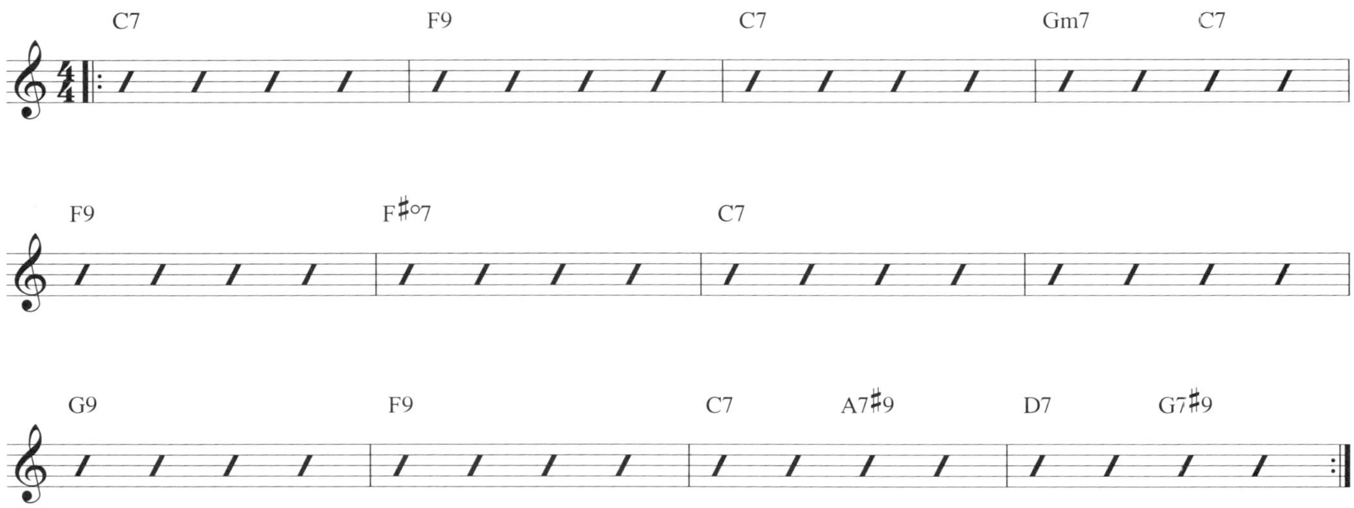

The F♯°7 chord really adds life to that measure and prevents things from feeling stale and stagnant.

Let's look into some ideas for measures 7 and 8. Instead of staying on the I chord (C7) for two measures, we can add in some interesting ii–V movements. Here is an example:

Example 13

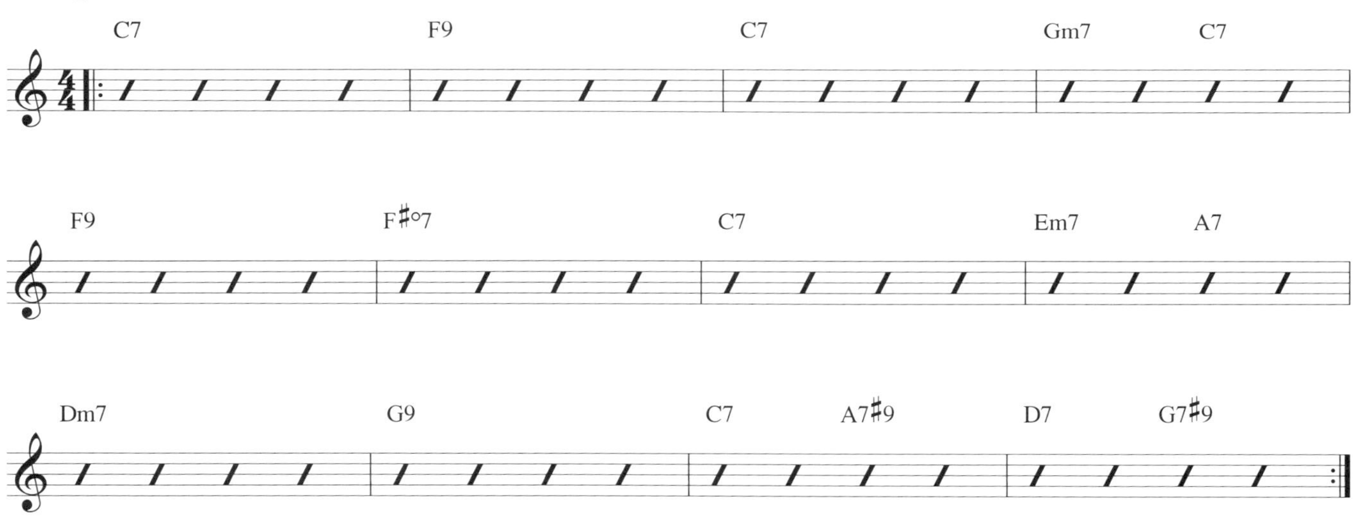

This truly takes the blues in a direction you might think of as jazz. This is not a coincidence. Jazz is very much an evolution of the blues into something more harmonically complex. The purpose of this book is really to show you the connections between these two idioms in a way that will hopefully help broaden your playing into new areas while still maintaining an inherent blues feel in your playing.

So far, we have explored the *major blues*. Now let's look at a basic *minor blues* progression. The minor blues consists of minor chords whereas the major blues uses major or dominant chords (such as C7, F7, etc.). The minor blues has a more somber feel, whereas the major blues has a more uplifting feel. Here is a basic minor blues:

Example 14

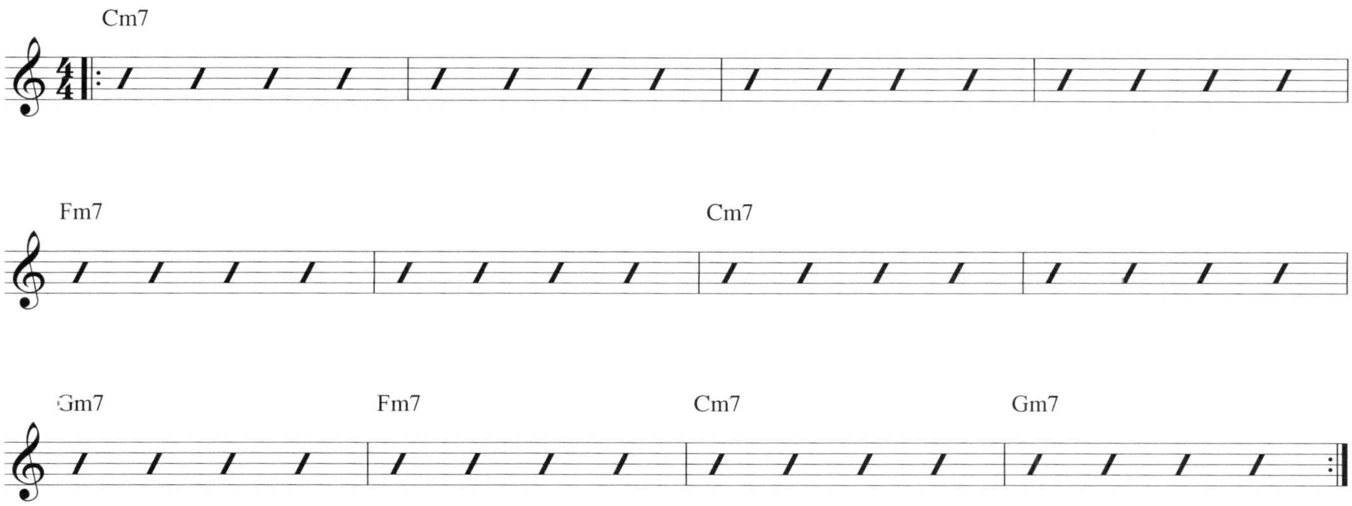

This example is as basic as you can get. Like with the other examples, we'll start with the bare bones and then build on it from there. The first change we can make is to make the last Gm7 a G7 chord as it is moving back to the Cm7. This is a V–i movement so that major 3rd in G7 acts as a leading tone (B) which pulls our ears more strongly back to the C note in the Cm7.

Here is that example:

Example 15

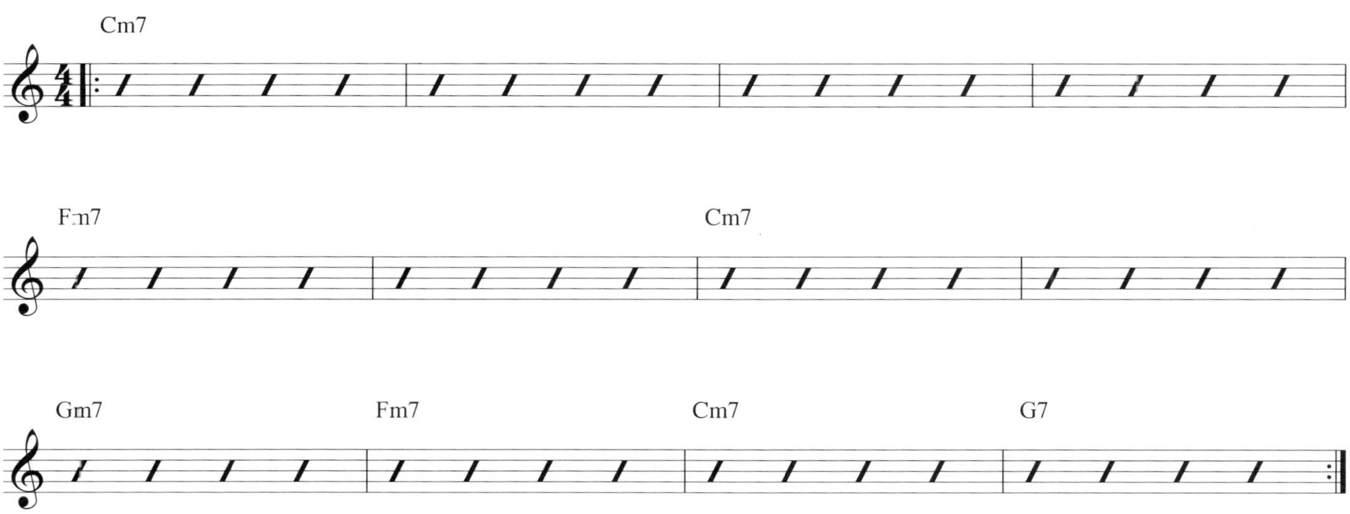

Now we can use the same "leading tone" approach when the fourth measure of Cm7 is moving into the Fm7 by turning into a C7 chord. It introduces an E note that leads our ears more directly to F in the following chord.

Example 16

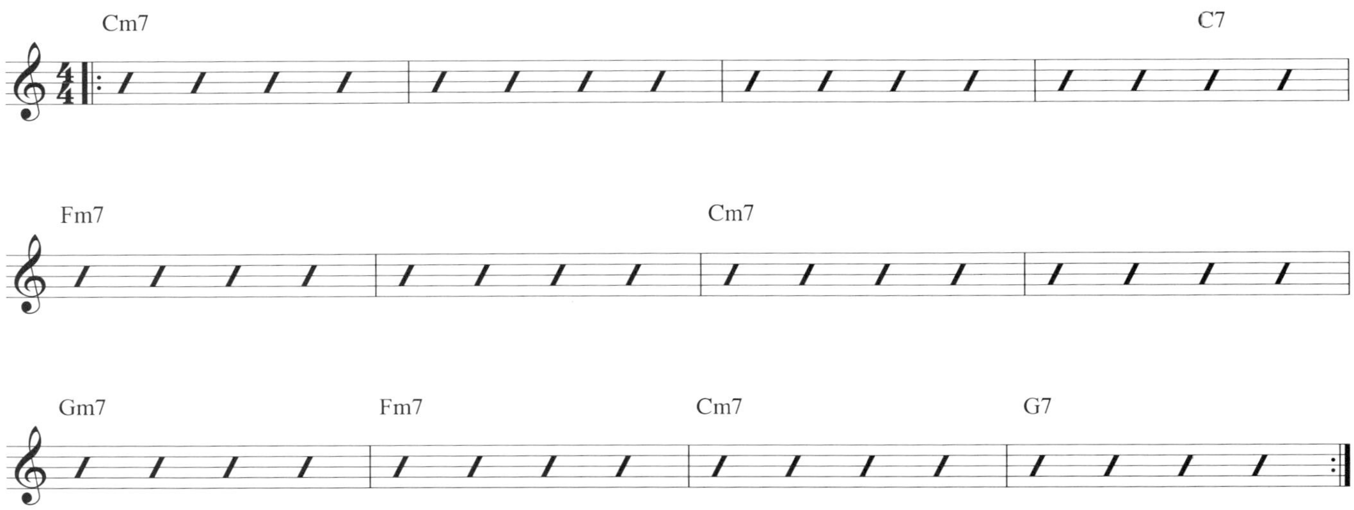

Here is another common trick in a minor blues. Instead of playing Gm7 and Fm7 (v and iv) in measures 9 and 10, we can borrow from the harmonic minor key and instead play ♭VI–V as seen in this example below:

Example 17

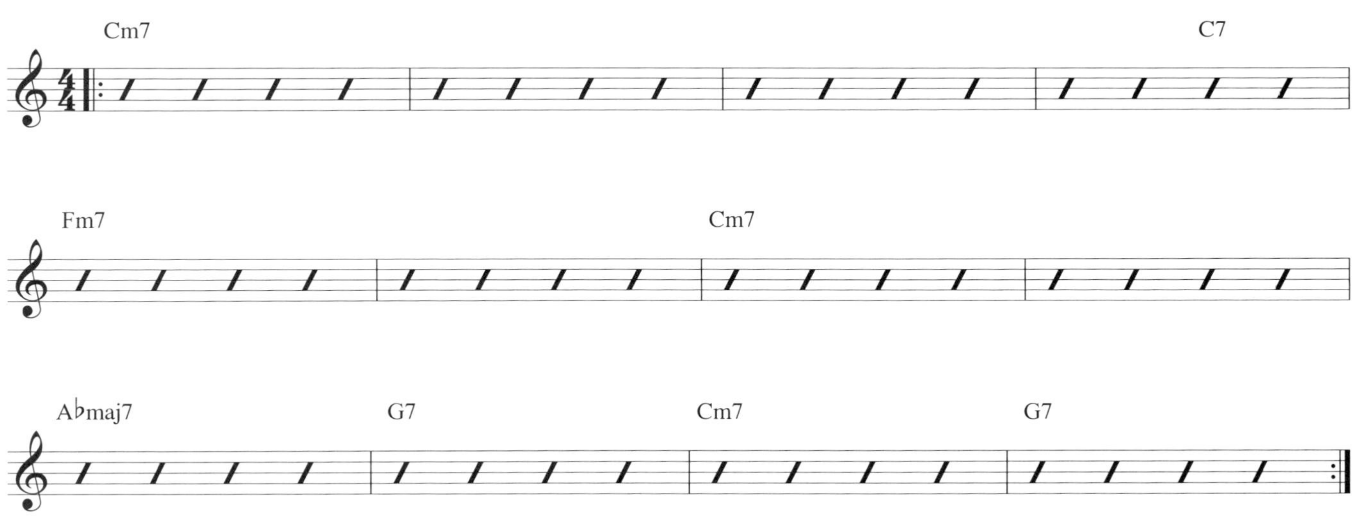

We see this kind of progression used in songs such as "The Thrill Is Gone" by B.B. King.

Another cool variation on this type of progression is to turn the ♭VI chord into a dominant chord (instead of being a major 7th). This gives us a very cool, bluesy feel. Let's check it out:

Example 18

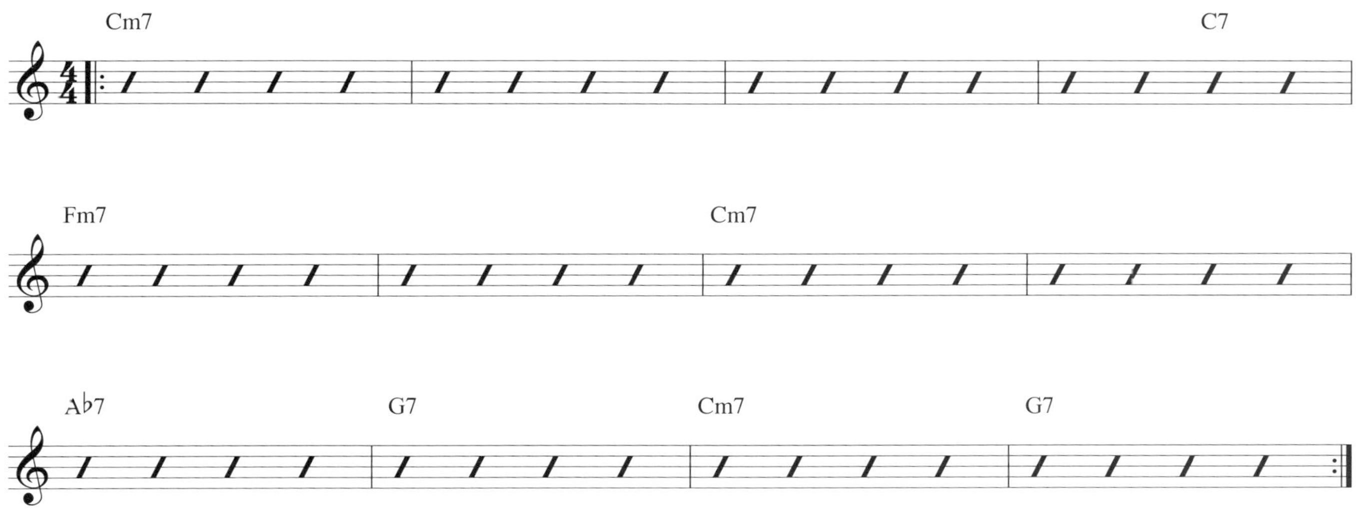

This simple and subtle change noticeably transforms the progression. The G♭ note (functioning as the ♭7 of the A♭7 chord) is highlighted, as it is the ♭5 in a C blues scale. That's really the characteristic sound of the blues scale.

Now let's talk about extending the chords with 9ths. Just as in the major blues, in the minor blues, we can extend our chords beyond the 7th (or minor 7th in this case).

- Here is the C minor scale: C–D–E♭–F–G–A♭–B♭.
- In terms of intervals, it looks like this: 1–2–♭3–4–5–♭6–♭7.

In the second octave, we get a 9th which translates to the 2nd in the next octave. We can simply add this to our minor 7th chord, transforming it into a minor 9 chord.

- Here is our minor 7th chord in terms of intervals: 1–♭3–5–♭7.
- Let's add the 9th to make it a minor 9th chord: 1–♭3–5–♭7–9.

We can do this to dominant chords as discussed earlier. If the chord is functioning as a V chord, we can make the extension altered (7♯9).

We can also extend the chord if it is a major 7th, like in bar 9 of Example 19. The chord is A♭maj7, but we can make it A♭maj9 as we extend the formula by using an A♭ major scale.

- Here is the formula for a major 7 chord: 1–3–5–7.
- And here is the formula for a major 9 chord: 1–3–5–7–9.

Now let's take these chord extensions and apply them to Example 19:

Example 19

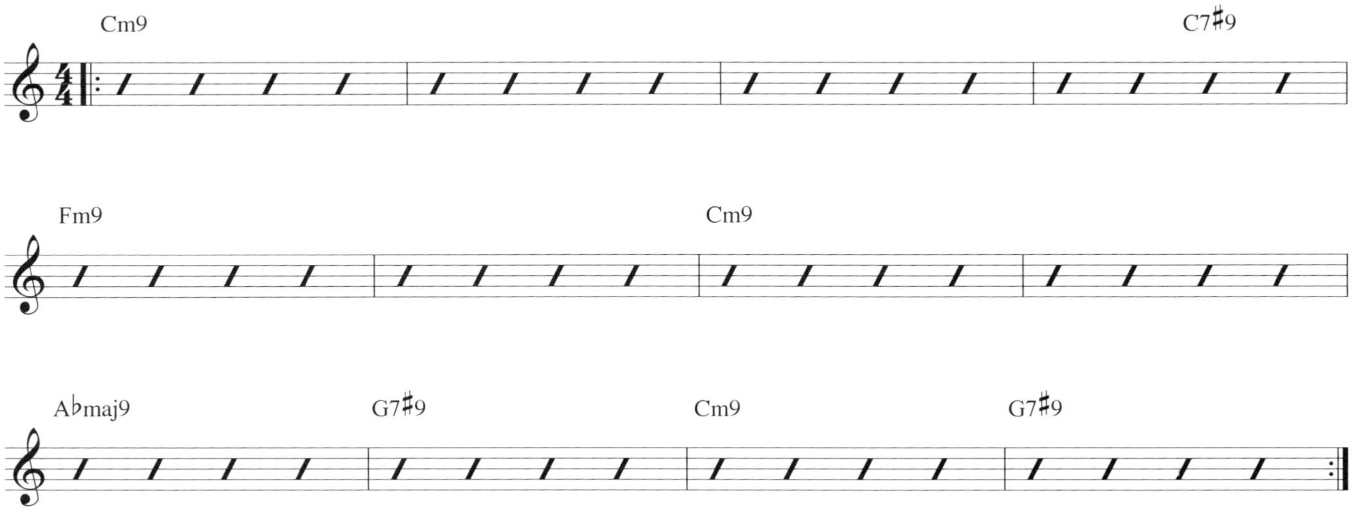

You may notice I used 7♯9 when applied to the C7 and not C9. This is because the C7 is functioning as the V chord of the Fm9 that comes after it. Whenever we add extensions to a functioning V dominant chord, we can alter them in order to give a stronger pull into the next chord. Now let's apply these same concepts to Example 20:

Example 20

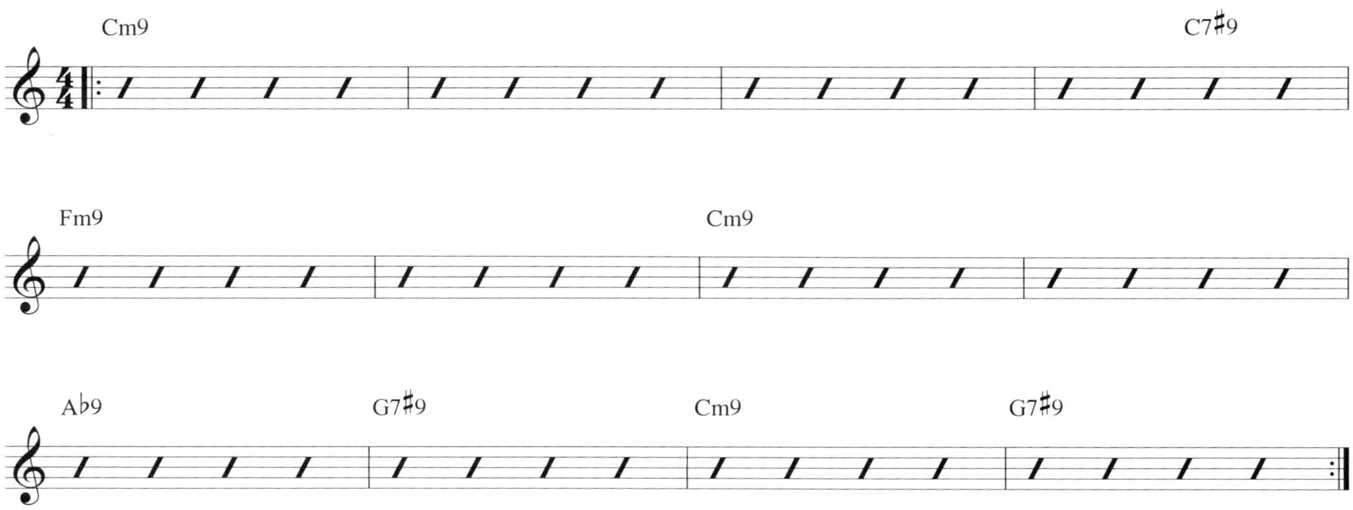

Here you will notice that in measure 9, I used A♭9. This is because the dominant chord, in this case, is not functioning as a V chord to the chord after it; therefore, I do not add any alterations and instead, keep it as a simple dominant 9 chord.

With all these examples, I have taken the point to explain the theoretical concepts behind the chord choices. In addition to learning these progressions, be sure to take the time to understand how they work and how even the most complex examples are really just an evolution of the basic blues progressions. You can use these in live situations in order to bring extra interest to your jam sessions.

Shell Voicings

I would like to wrap up this chapter by outlining some basic chord shapes we can use on the guitar. I like to avoid the typical five- and six-string chord voicings when playing the blues, as they tend to be too jangly and not punchy enough for most blues situations.

Here is a C7 chord in what we call a *shell voicing*. These shell voicings contain only the essential notes of the chord (the root, 3rd, and 7th). You'll notice we have omitted the 5th, as it only serves to support the root and doesn't add any real color when left unaltered. This version of C7 has the root note on the low E string:

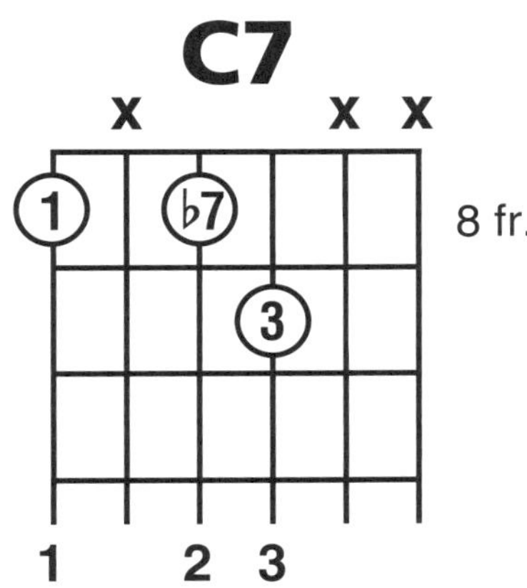

Our root note is on the eighth fret. If we wanted to transpose this shape into another key and make it F7, we would simply need to move the shape so the root note is F and not C. This means we would need to move it all the way from the eighth fret to the first fret. In order to keep C7 and F7 closer together, it is better to have another shape with its root on the A string. Here is C7 with an A-string root:

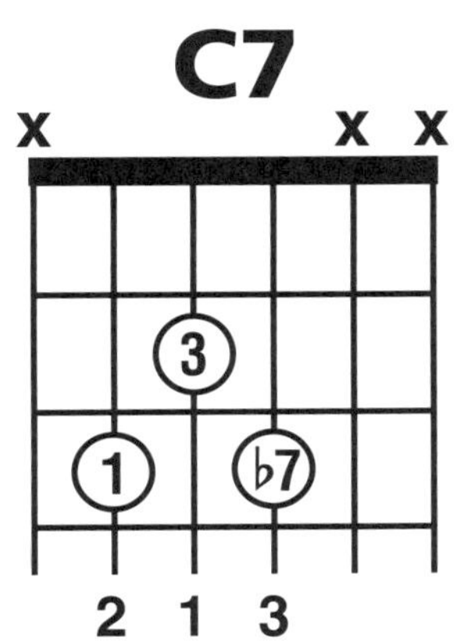

This shape is C7 because its root note is on the A string, third fret which is indeed the note of C. If we want to make this shape F7, we would simply move the entire shape to the eighth fret, making the chord F7 by virtue of the fact that the root is now F and not C. Here are C7 and F7 placed at the eighth and seventh frets, respectively, using the shapes we have learned so far:

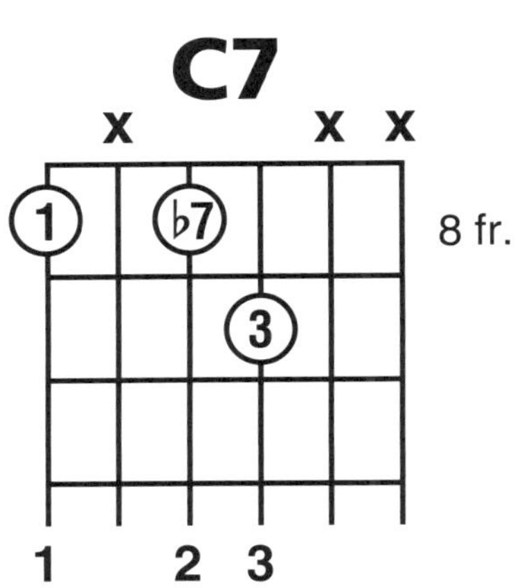

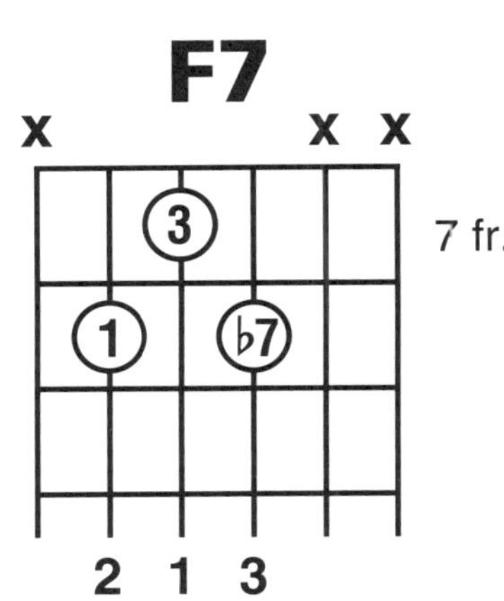

It is also possible to use these two shapes in reverse and play them around the third and first frets, respectively:

C7

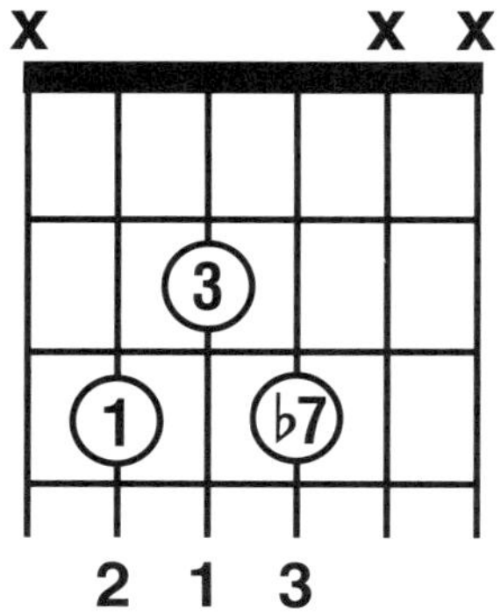

F7

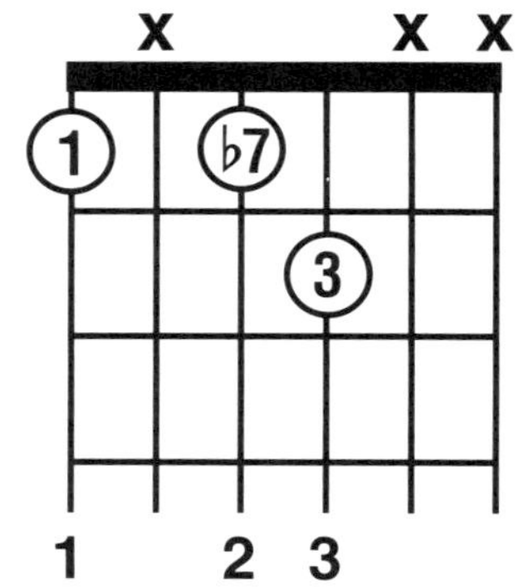

If we consider that, in most situations, the bass player will be playing the root note, we can leave out the root entirely and still have a very clear picture of the chord. This leaves us with just the 3rd and ♭7 intervals. What is even more amazing is you will notice they often just move in half-step increments (one fret). To move from C7 to F7, we simply move our 3rd and ♭7 down one fret (the root is labeled for reference but should not be played):

C7

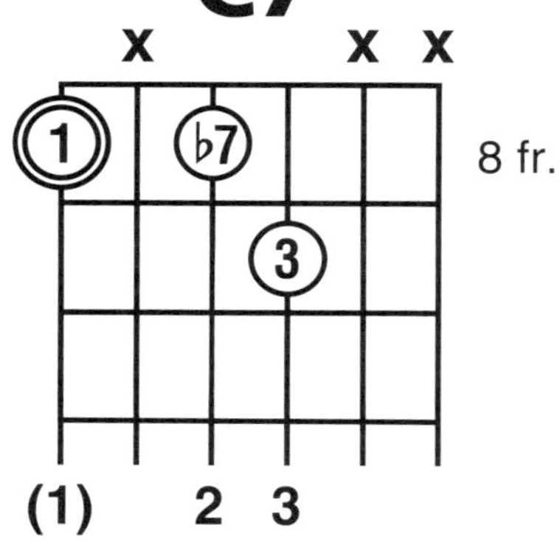

F7

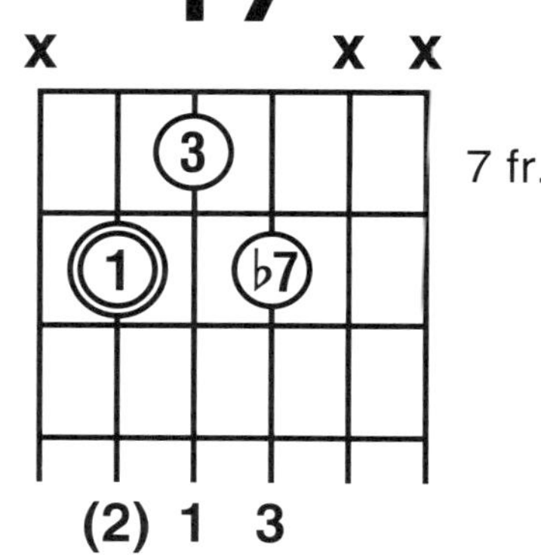

Here we can see that the ♭7 and 3rd in C7 only have to shift down by one fret to become the 3rd and ♭7 of F7 (notice that the intervals invert). If we add G7 into the mix, we can see that G7 is one fret higher than C7 and two frets higher than F7:

C7

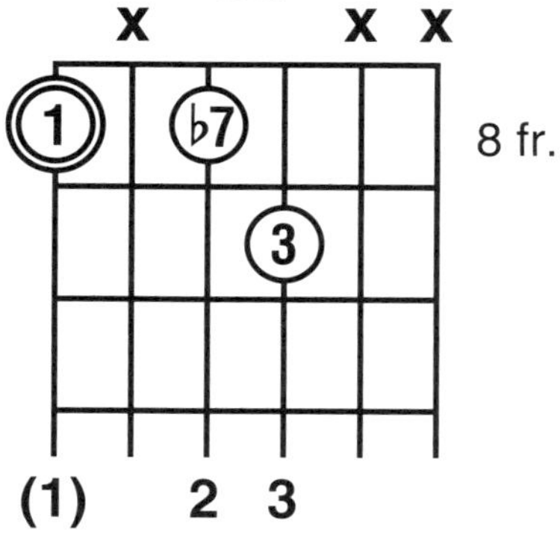

F7

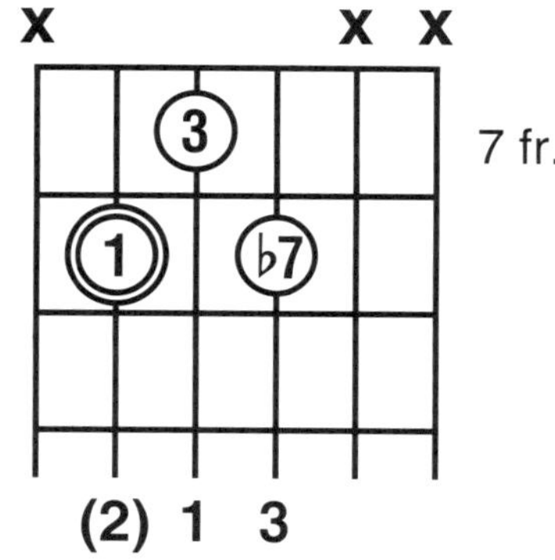

G7

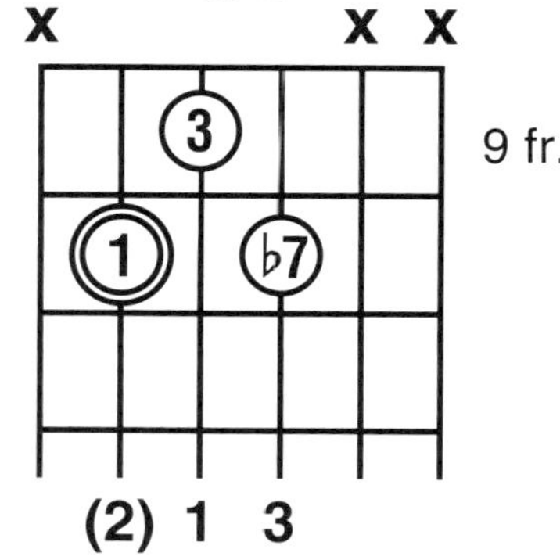

We just learned the chord tones in one position around the eighth fret. We can now move these shapes down to the third fret. Here is that example:

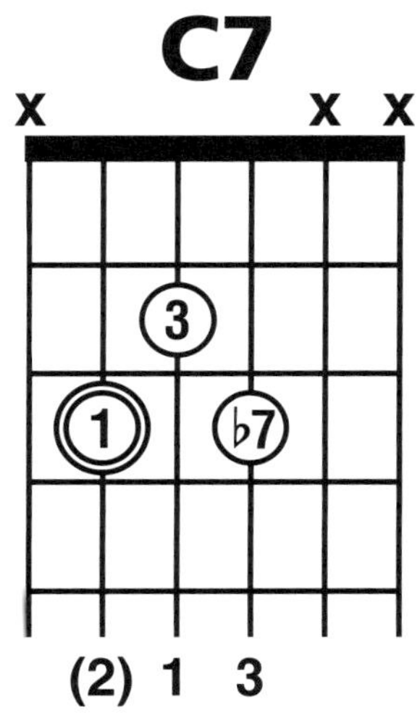

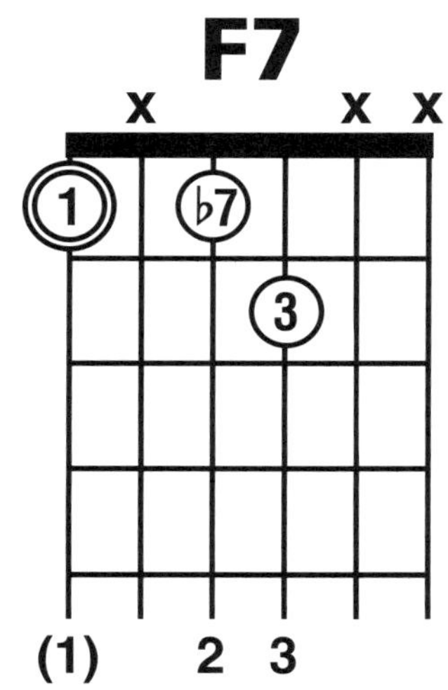

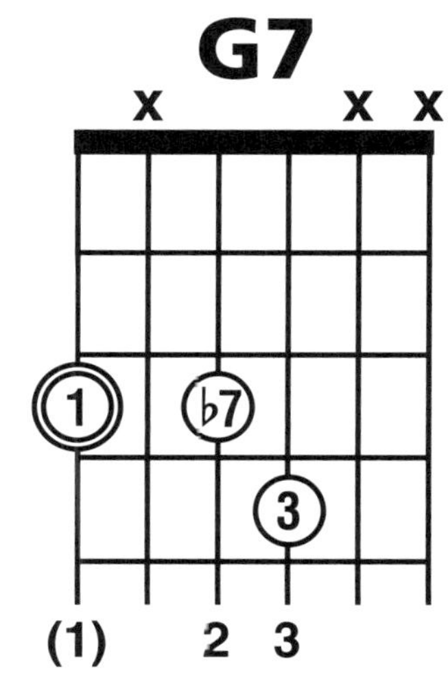

These intervals (3rd and ♭7) are referred to as the *guide tones*. It is important to visualize where the root would be even though we are not playing it. This gives us the necessary knowledge to transpose these guide tones into any key. The wonderful thing is once we understand what these intervals are, we can easily translate these guide tones into a number of different chord types.

The formula for a dominant 7th chord is 1–3–5–♭7. We omitted the 5th, as it is merely a support for the root and adds no distinct color. We also omitted the root since the bass player can take care of that. We were left with just the 3rd and ♭7 (guide tones). It stands to reason we could do the same thing with minor 7th chords and major 7th chords.

The formula for minor 7th chords is 1–♭3–5–♭7. We can leave out the root and 5th as we did with the dominant 7th chords, leaving us with ♭3 and ♭7. All we need to do is lower the 3rd in our previous shapes by one fret and keep the ♭7 where it is. This method helps us to understand the distinct differences between different chord types, which is often just one fret!

Here are the shapes for minor 7th guide tones around the eighth fret and sixth frets, depending on the chord:

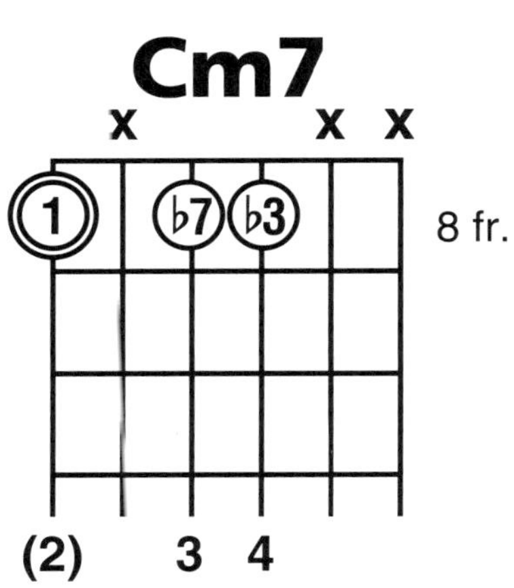

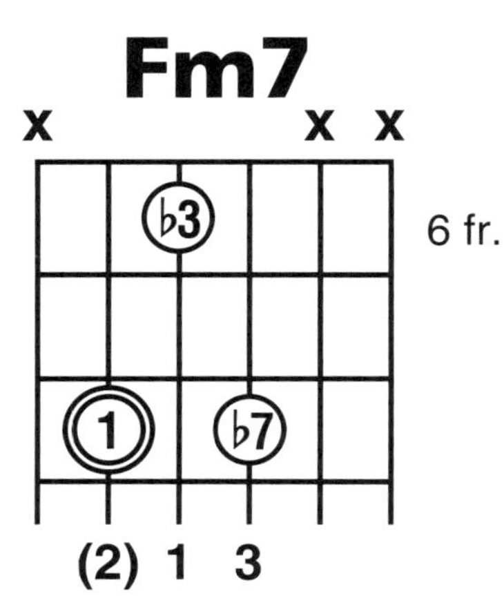

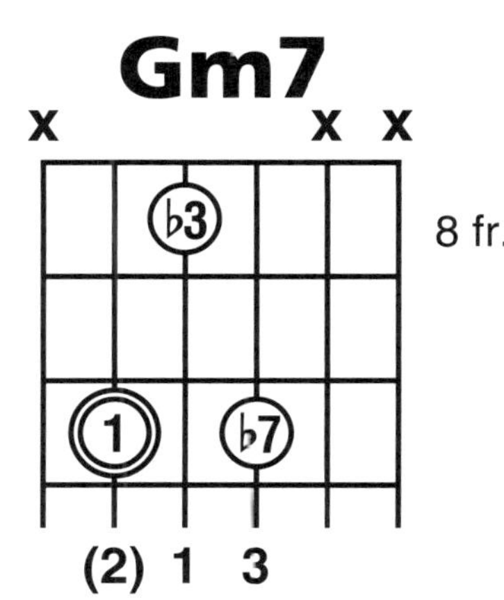

And here are the minor 7th guide tones around the third fret:

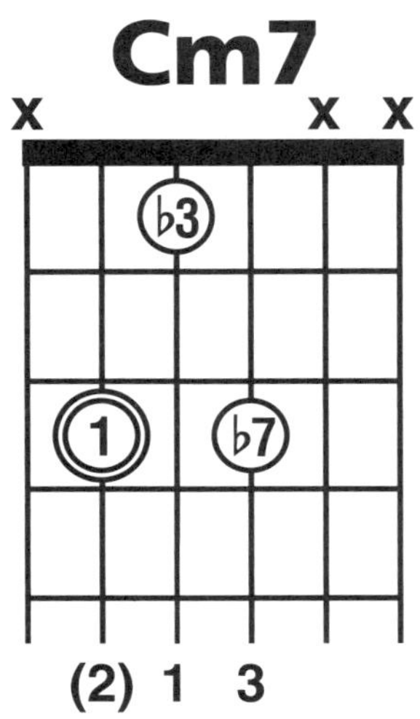

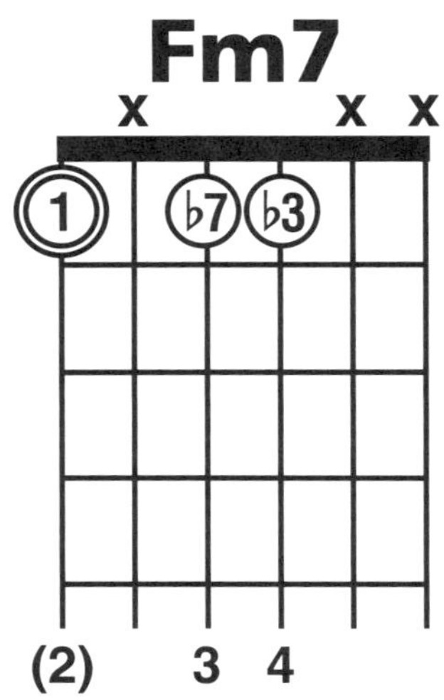

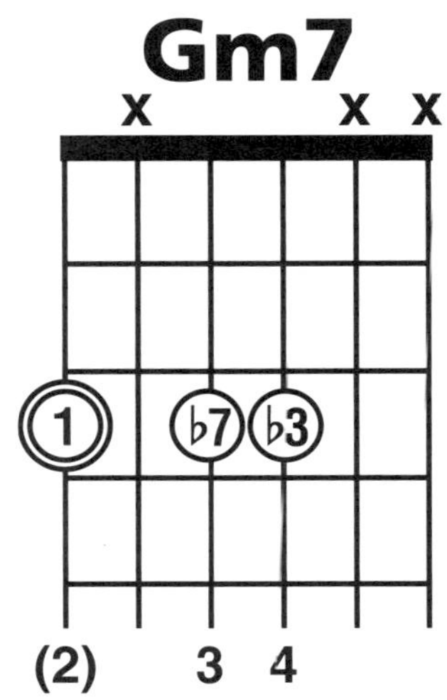

If we consider major 7th chords, we realize that the formula is also only one note different from a dominant 7th chord. Here is the formula for a major 7th chord: 1–3–5–7. The only difference from the dominant 7th chord is that the 7th itself is no longer flatted. Therefore, if we locate the ♭7 in the dominant 7th chord and simply raise it by one fret, we have a major 7th chord. Here is the major 7th guide tone shape built around an E-string root:

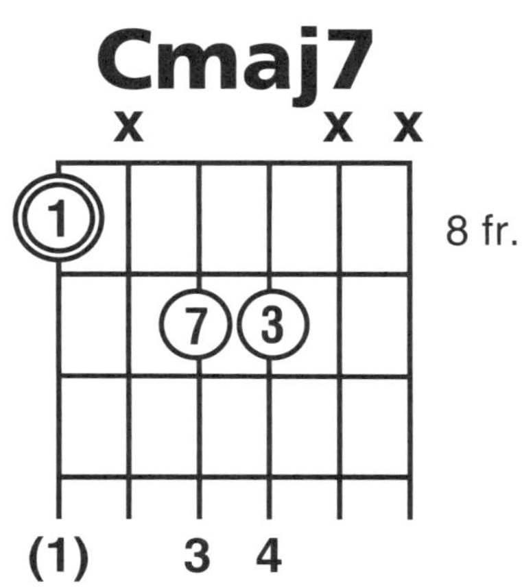

And here is the major 7th shape built from an A-string root:

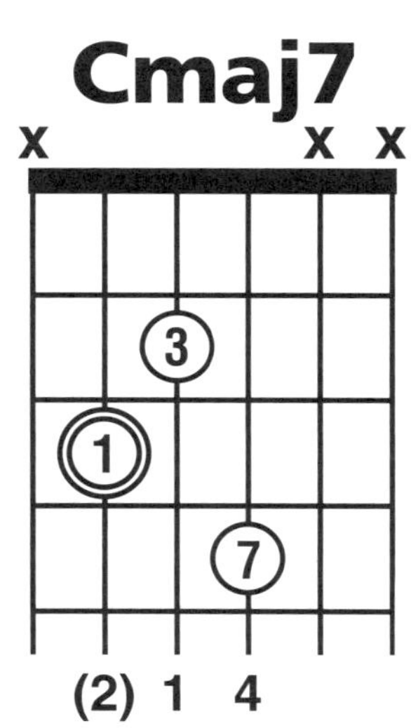

Now let's look at an example of the minor blues from Example 18 which uses some of the chord voicings we have talked about so far. I have included the root note in these shapes:

Example 21

This is a great example of how less is more when performing a rhythm part in a band situation. Often, we are trying to make room for other instruments while still outlining the harmony and yet not dominating the space sonically.

Here is an example of a major blues (Example 4) using these same types of shell chords:

Example 22

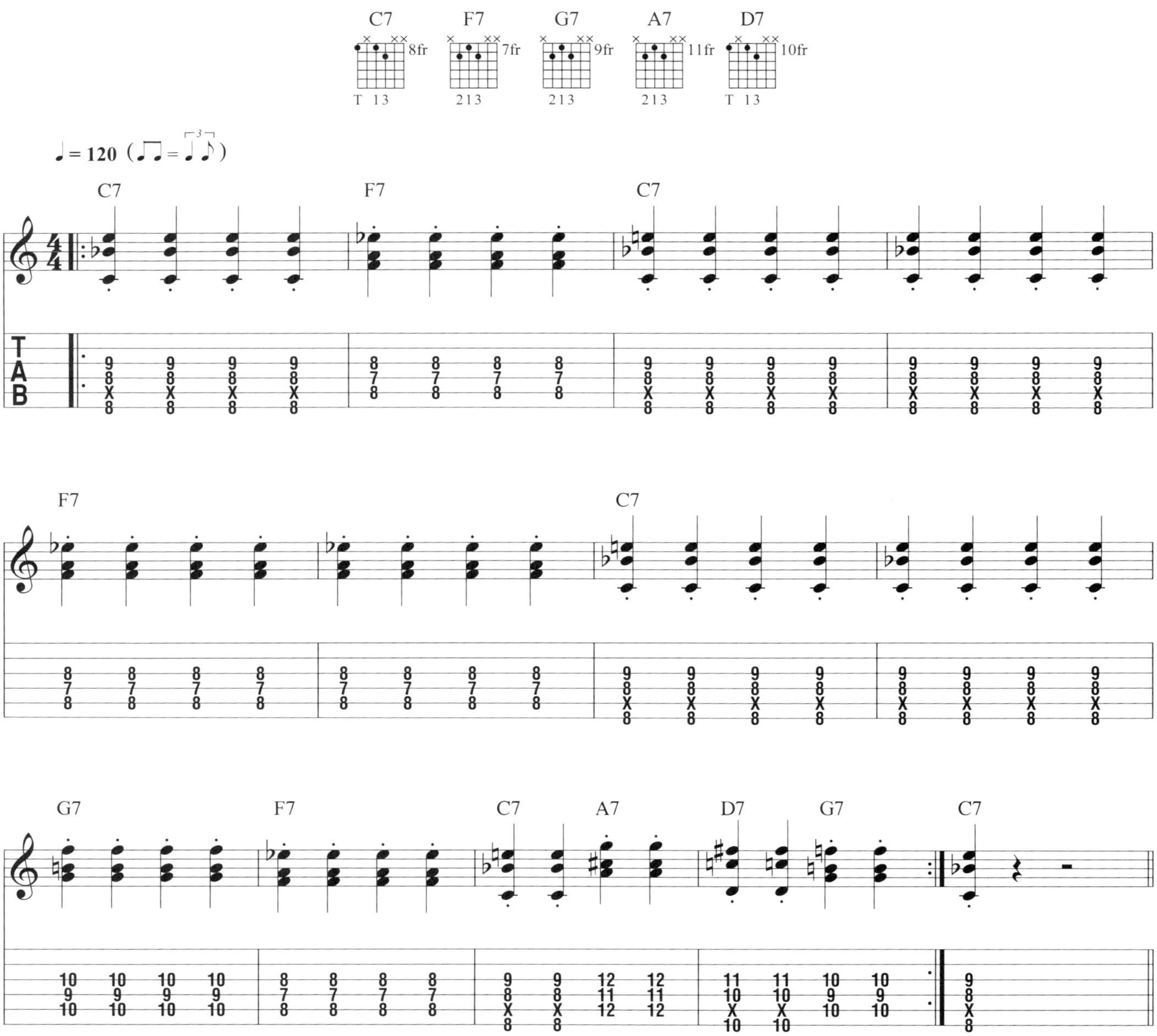

Adding Extensions to Shell Chords

Now that we have looked at the basic shell chords, you may be wondering about extended chords such as 9ths. The great news is we now have the basic skeleton of the chord with the shell chord shapes. All we need to do is add that additional 9th, and we have the 9th chords formed. First, let's see what a 9th looks like.

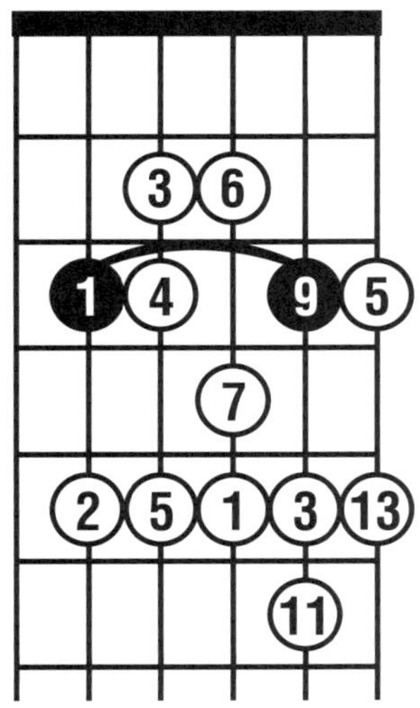

This is a C major scale with its root on the A string. It spans over two octaves, and the labeling includes *compound intervals*. As mentioned before, once we reach the second-octave root, we start naming the intervals as 9 for 2nd, 11 for 4th, etc. So a 9th is simply the 2nd in the next octave. If we were to add this 9th interval to our dominant 7th shell chord, we end up with a 9th chord. Here is a C9 chord. Notice it is simply a C7 shell chord with the addition of the 9th interval:

C9

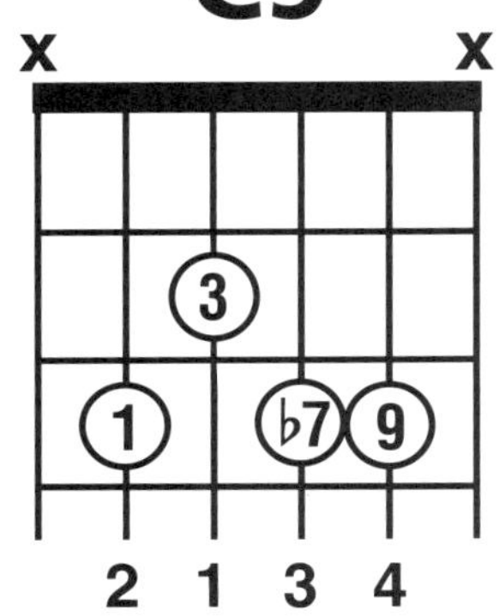

Let's take this same approach and apply it to the minor 7th shell chord with an A-string root:

Cm9

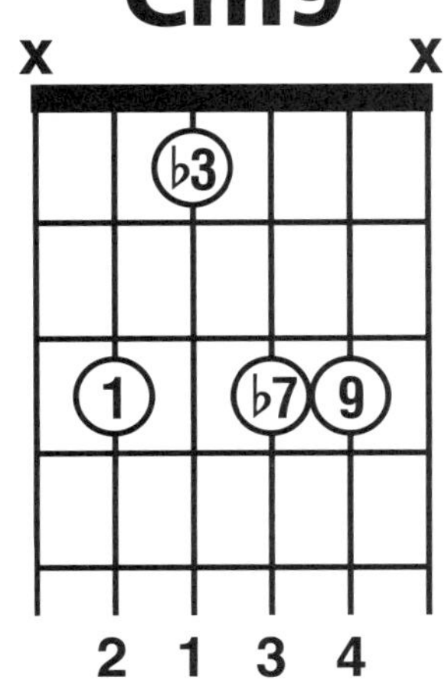

Now let's do the same thing to the major 7th shell chord. When we add the 9th, it becomes a major 9 chord:

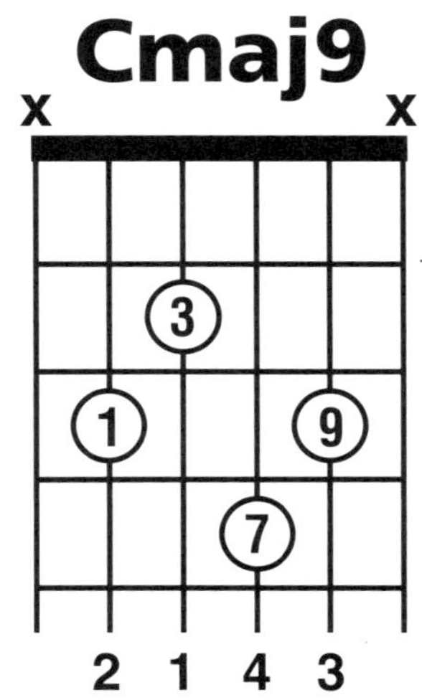

That concludes the 9th with an A-string root. These are very common voicings that are applicable for many styles.

Now let's look at some voicings with an E-string root. We run into the issue of them sounding too muddy if we simply use the same voicings transposed to the lower strings, so we often have to omit certain notes in order for them to work tonally as well as musically. The most common thing is for the 3rd interval to sound way too muddy between the E and A strings. Let's look at a common voicing for C9, and I will talk you through the rationale behind this.

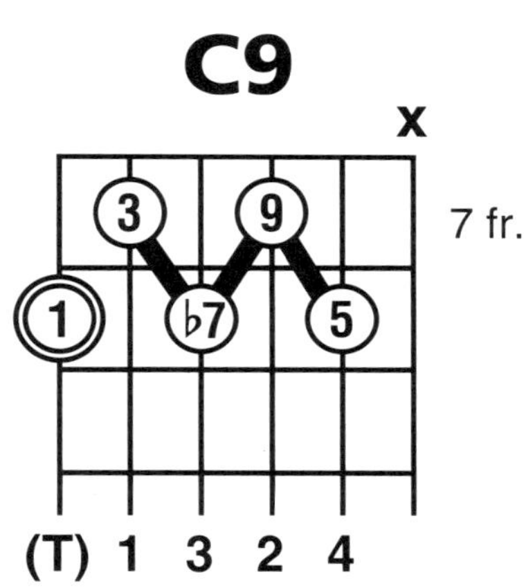

As you can see, the root note is shown for reference purposes only. You could play it with the thumb, but it's really not necessary. The chord shape itself has the 3rd as its lowest note, leaving the root-note duties to the bass player. This makes for a clearer and more spread-out sound. The eagle eyed among you may notice that the 1–3–♭7 would make the same shape as the shell chord that started on the A string in previous examples. It can sound a little muddy if we play the root note, so I prefer not to play it most of the time. If we just play the ♭7, 9th, and 5th, we can slide those up two frets to get some classic blues chord riffs.

Example 23

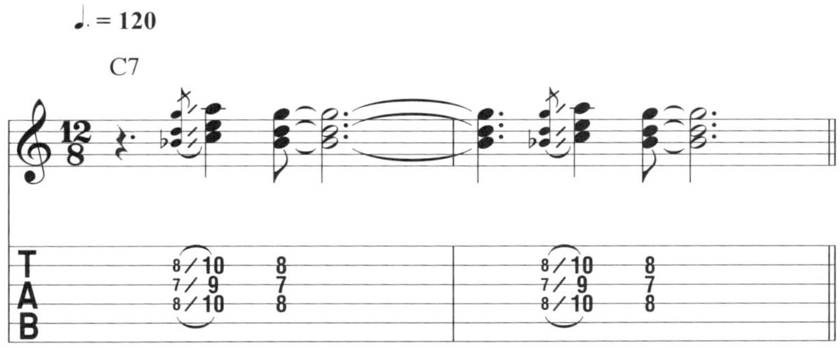

This is a classic blues riff that you can use instead of simply playing a C7 or C9 chord. These kinds of riffs spice up your blues chord playing to create more interest.

We can transfer this blues riff over to the top three strings as an extension of our 9th shape we saw with the A-string root. Here is that shape again with the 5th added on the high E string:

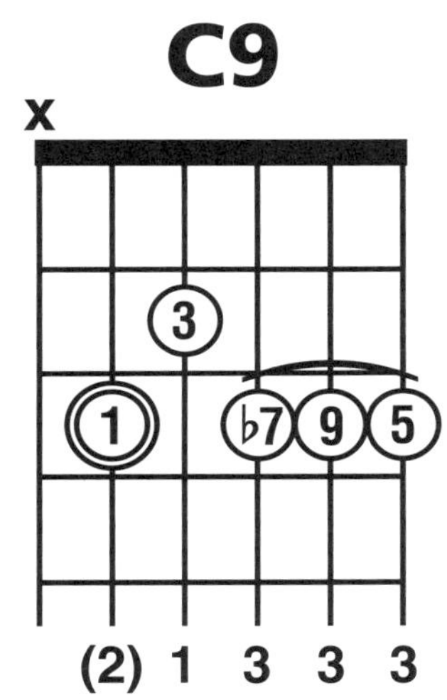

If we look at the top three strings (♭7, 9, and 5), you will notice a straight row of notes. We can also slide these three notes around to create the same exact riff that we saw with the E-string root C9:

Example 24

Now with this riff available to us on both string sets, we can easily apply it to a 12-bar blues. It's important to see the chord shape that this riff has originated from and see where the riff starts in relation to the root of each chord. If we do not take the time to learn and see the root, then it will be difficult for us to transpose any of these riffs. I cannot emphasize enough the importance of learning to play things in as many keys as possible.

Let's check out this cool blues example:

Example 25

It sounds simple enough. Hopefully by now you have a clear understanding of where this blues riff sits in relation to the root and the original chord.

Now let's look at some of the other E-string root chords. First, we'll examine two versions of Cm9, each with an E-string root:

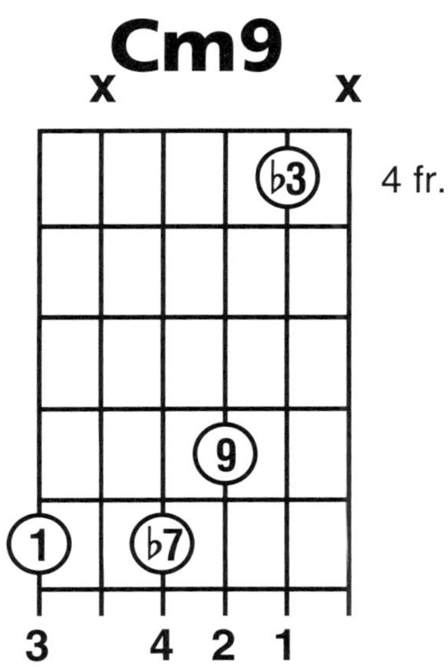

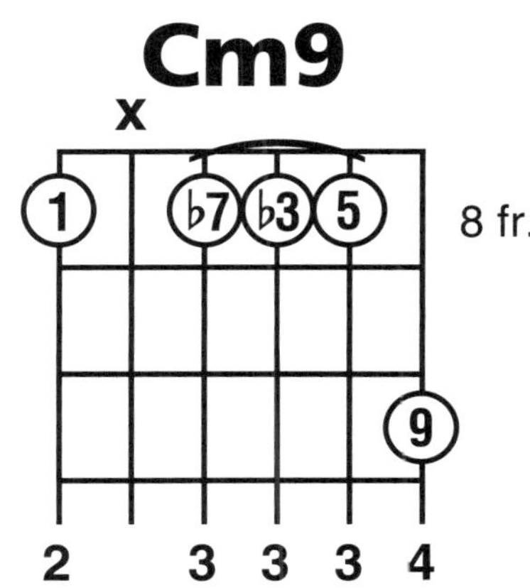

These two versions of the Cm9 chord both have their roots placed on the low E string. There is something cool about having the 9th and ♭3rd sound just a half step apart instead of placing them in different octaves. Having them closer together is something more akin to a piano voicing. I really love the sound of the first one, but it is a bit of a stretch for many players. For ease and convenience, the second voicing is closer together in terms of frets, making it easier to play.

Now let's look at some major 9 chord voicings with an E-string root:

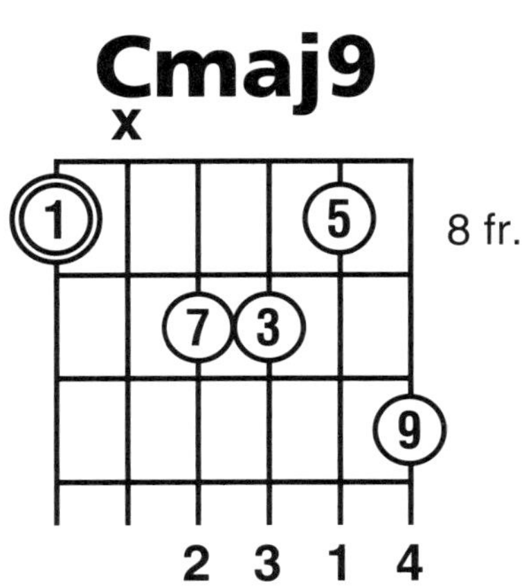

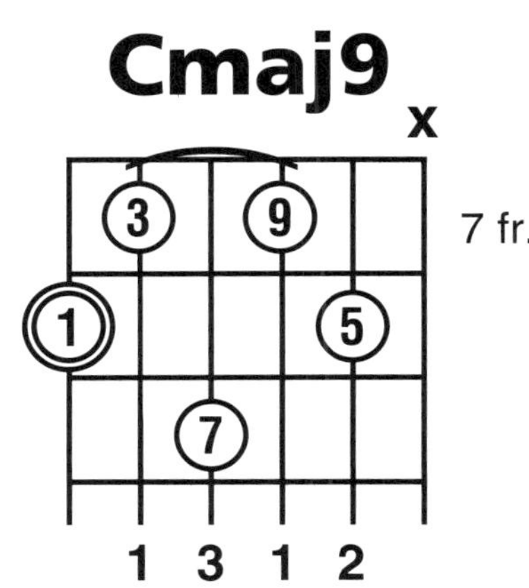

I have made the root optional in these two chord voicings, as it is difficult to play them and not totally necessary either. All of the chord voicings so far should be memorized and applied within a blues context wherever you see fit.

Other chord types include 7♯9, 7♯5, 7sus4, and 13. Here are some chord charts for them using both E-string and A-string roots:

C7♯9

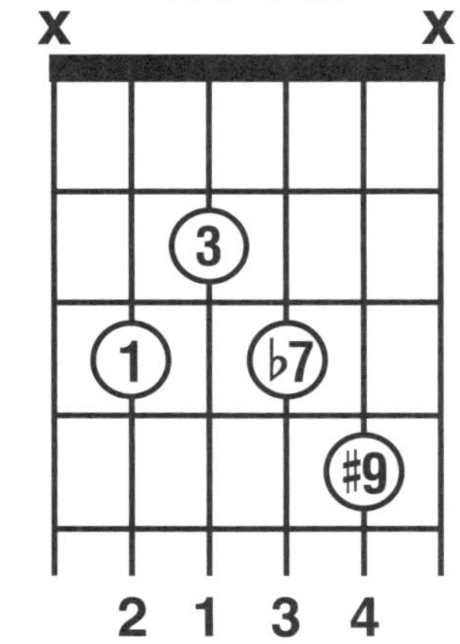

C7sus4

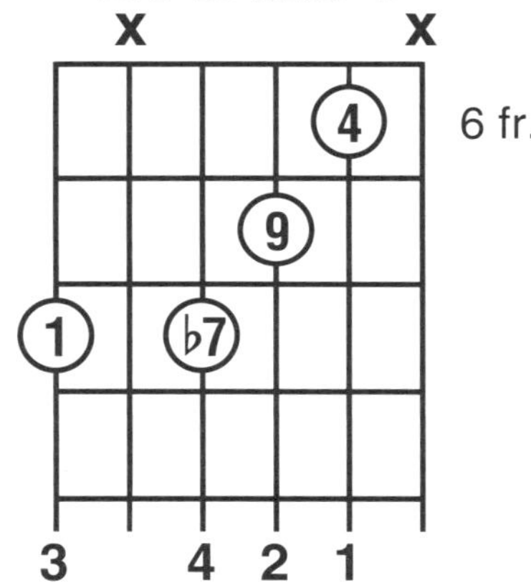

C13

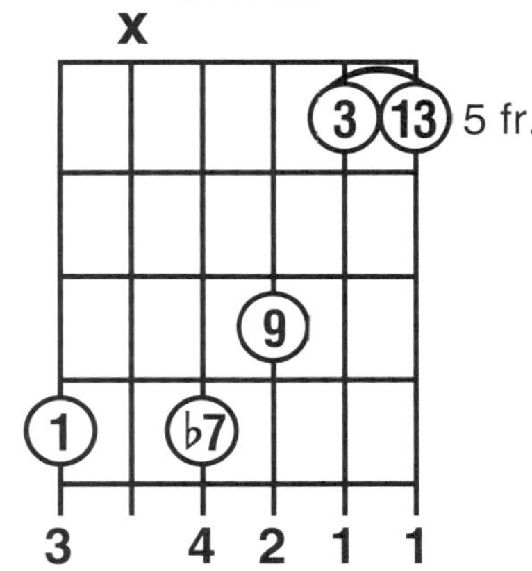

C7♯5

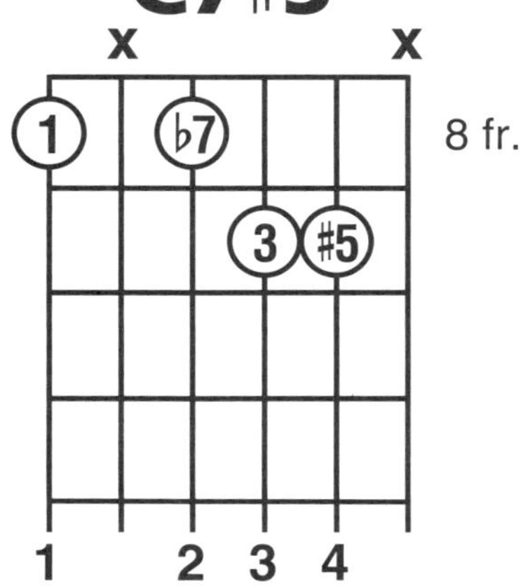

C13

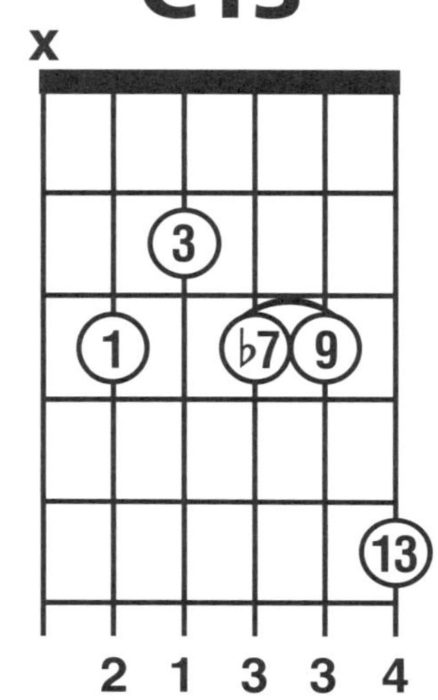

C7sus4

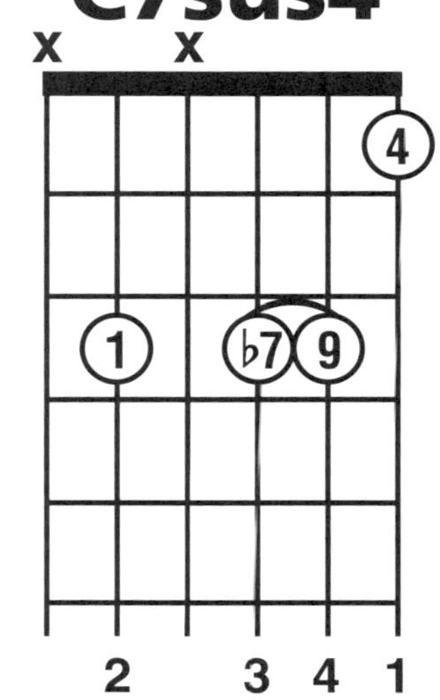

C13

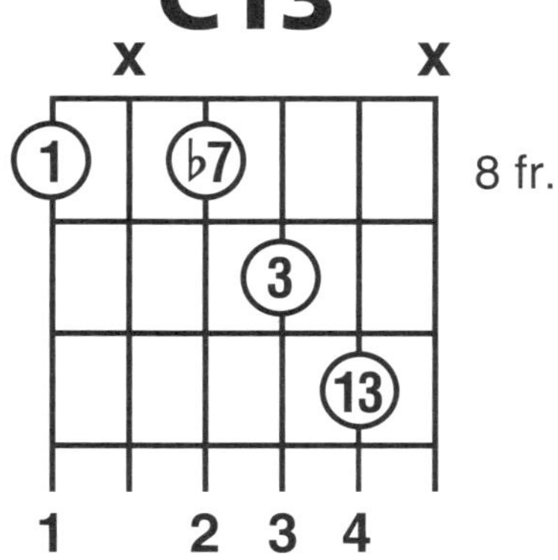

C13

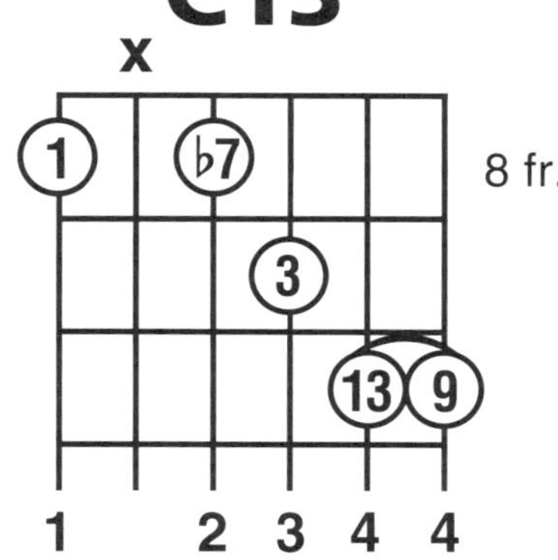

C7♯9♯5

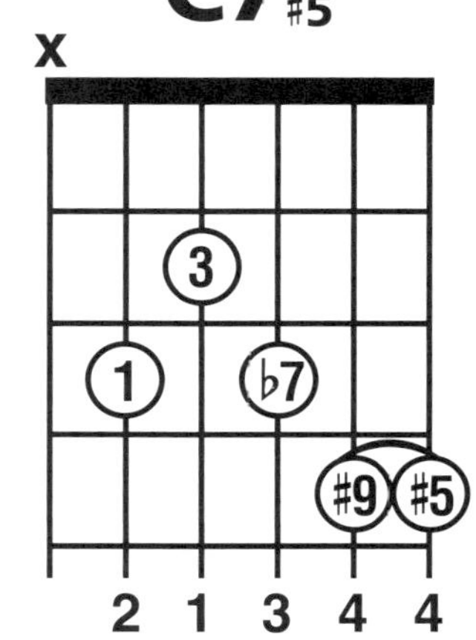

It is important that you understand where each of these chord types can be applied. Often, the best way to do that is to simply learn progressions and observe the application of chord types within them. I have laid out some of the basic rules in this book, and hopefully, you will gain an understanding as you work through the given examples.

I am now going to show some examples of blues progressions that can contain some of these interesting chord voicings. Let's go ahead and take a look:

C Minor Blues

Example 26

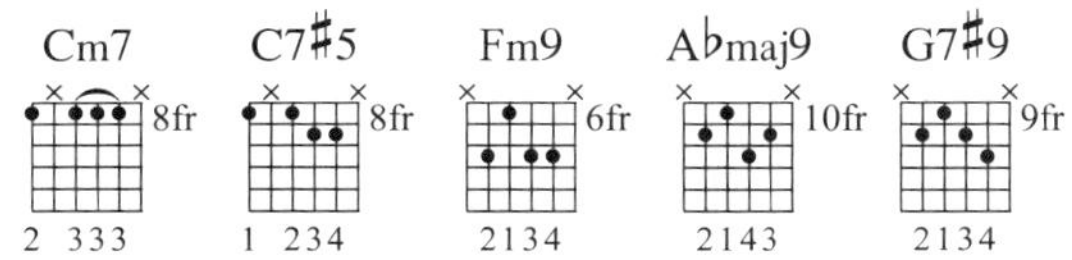

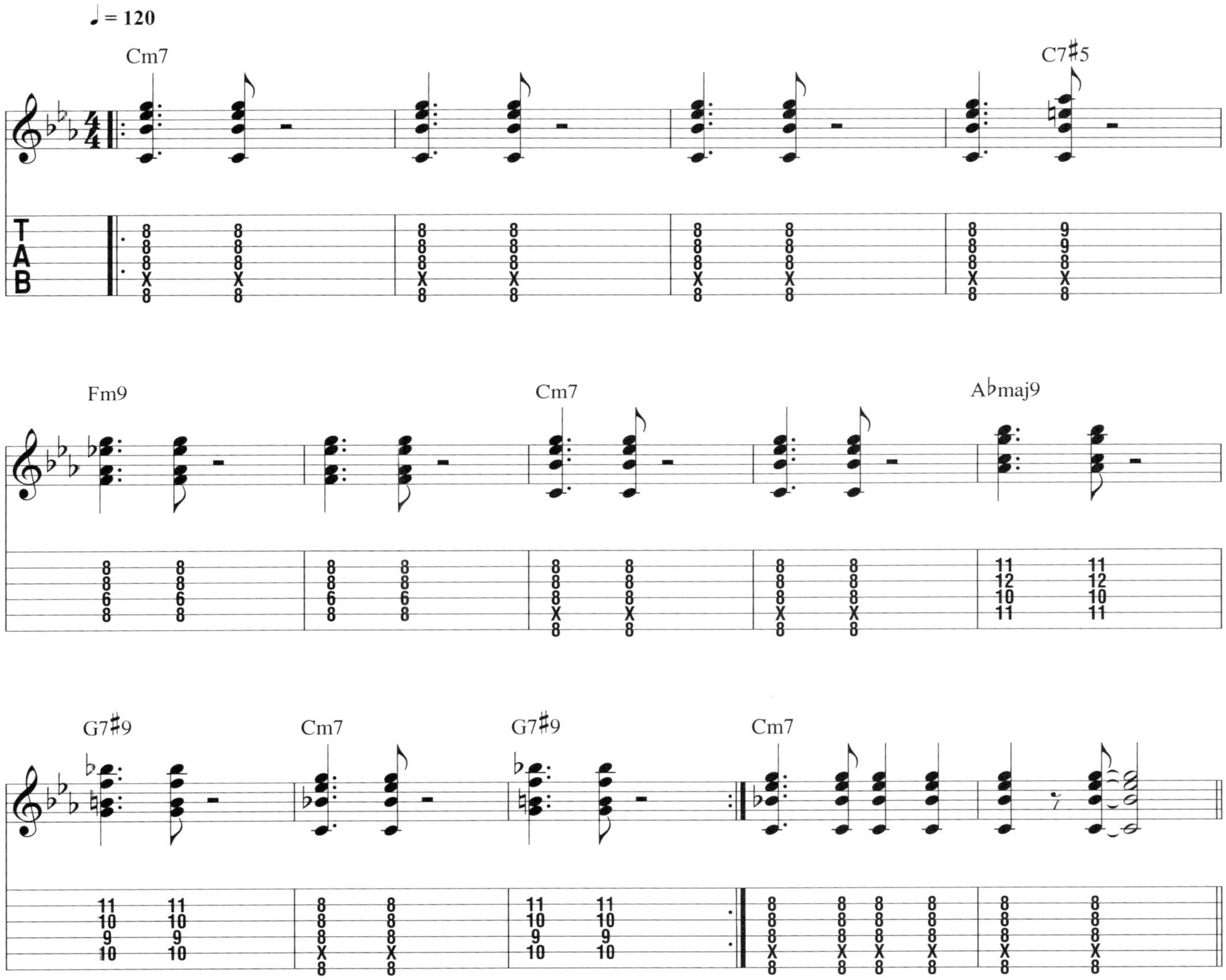

This C minor blues makes use of several of the extended chords we have learned and puts them into a musical context. There is also a slight variation on this blues where we make the ♭VI major 9 chord into a dominant 9 chord. Check out the next example to see how this small change brings a nice flavor to a minor blues progression.

C Minor Blues (with ♭VI dominant)

Example 27

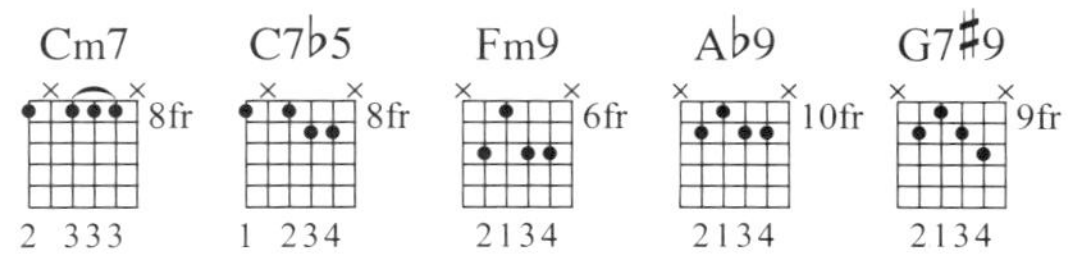

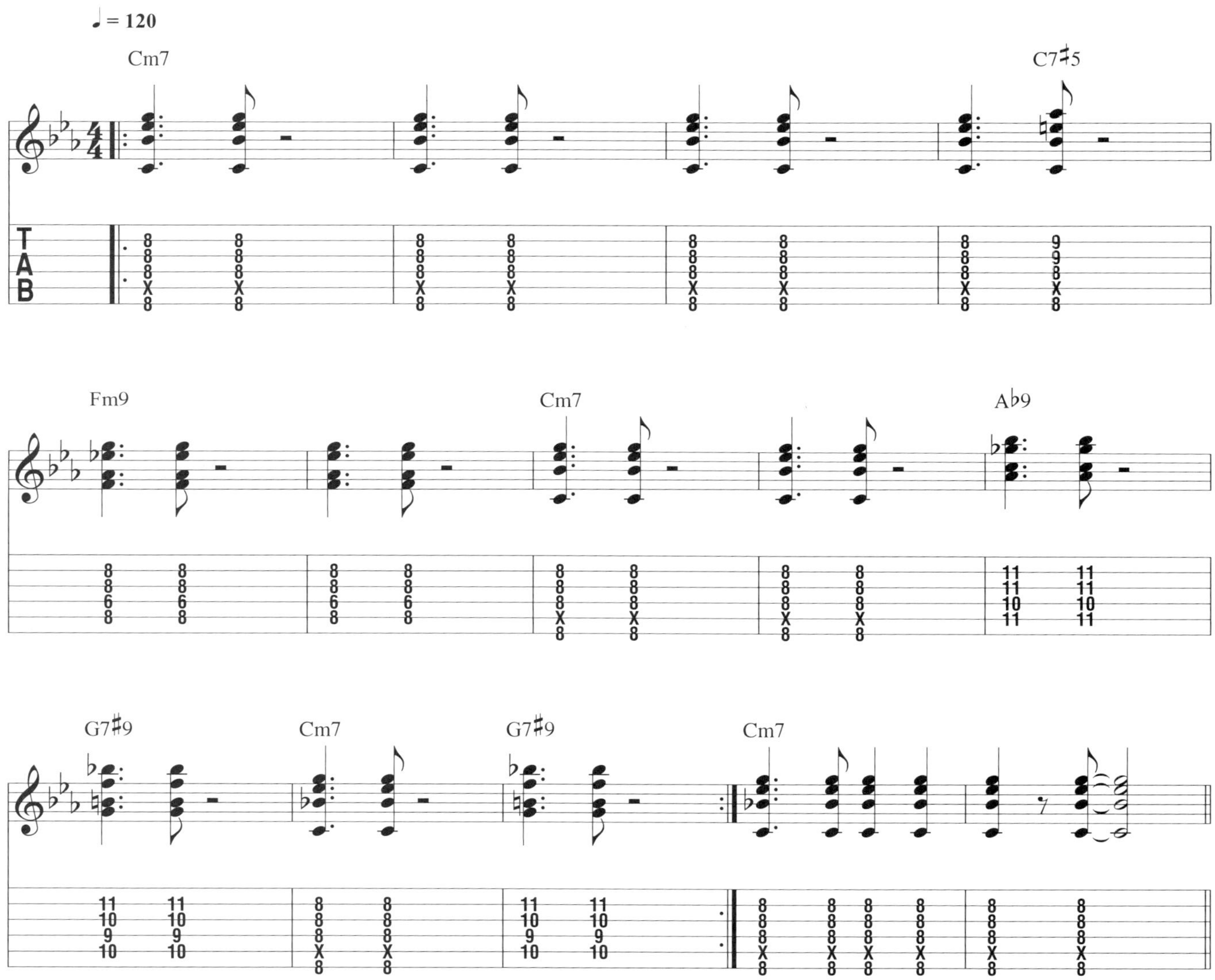

This small change makes an effective and dramatic impact to the bluesy feel of the progression. The G♭ note, working as the ♭7 of the A♭9 chord, really brings out the sound of the G♭ blue note in a C blues scale. As mentioned before, this scale is synonymous with the blues sound. Now let's look at a blues in G that contains a ton of the extended chords we learned:

Jazzy Blues

Example 28

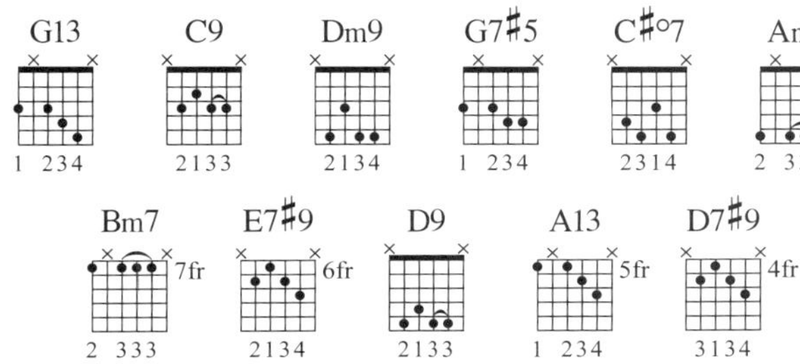

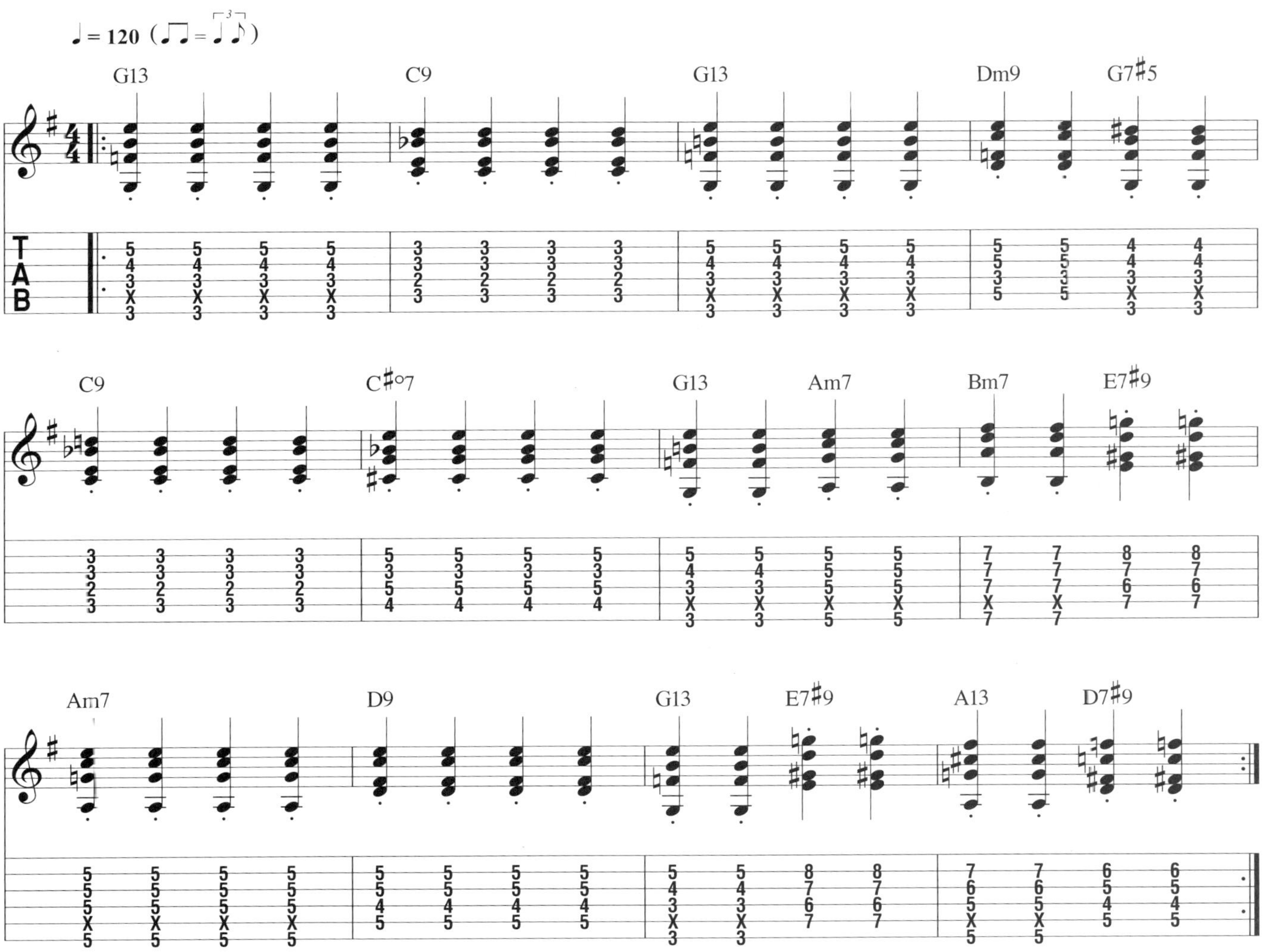

This is a more extreme it terms of all the extensions we added in there. It starts with simply replacing the G7 with a G13. We can always extend the chords within each category. For example, G7, G9, G7sus4, and G13 are all dominant chords and can be used in place of each other. I threw in the quick change in measure 2 and used C9 instead of the standard C7 that would be seen in a basic blues. In measure 4, I used a ii–V progression, which was the ii–V of the C9 chord. As already mentioned, even though the C9 is the IV chord in the context of the key of

G, we can imagine it to be the temporary I chord and lead into it, using its ii and V chords. This is a very effective approach in that measure as it leads our ears more strongly into that IV (C9) chord and breaks the monotony of staying on one chord for so long. In measure 6, I introduced a ♯IV diminished chord. This is effective when going from the IV to the I chord. We can introduce it in between for a stronger pull back to the I from the IV. In measures 7 and 8, I introduce some interest by adding extra chords instead of the usual approach of sitting on the I chord for two bars. Instead, I added ii, iii, and VI7, which then acts as the V chord to measure 9, where we land on the ii chord. This leads nicely to the V chord in measure 10. Finally, we concluded with a I–VI–II–V progression to end things. I chose to make every other chord a 7♯9, as they are acting as the V chord to the chords that follow them. Hopefully, this opens your ears to what is possible in a blues progression.

Now let's look at a blues that uses dominant 7sus4 chords:

Modern Blues

Example 29

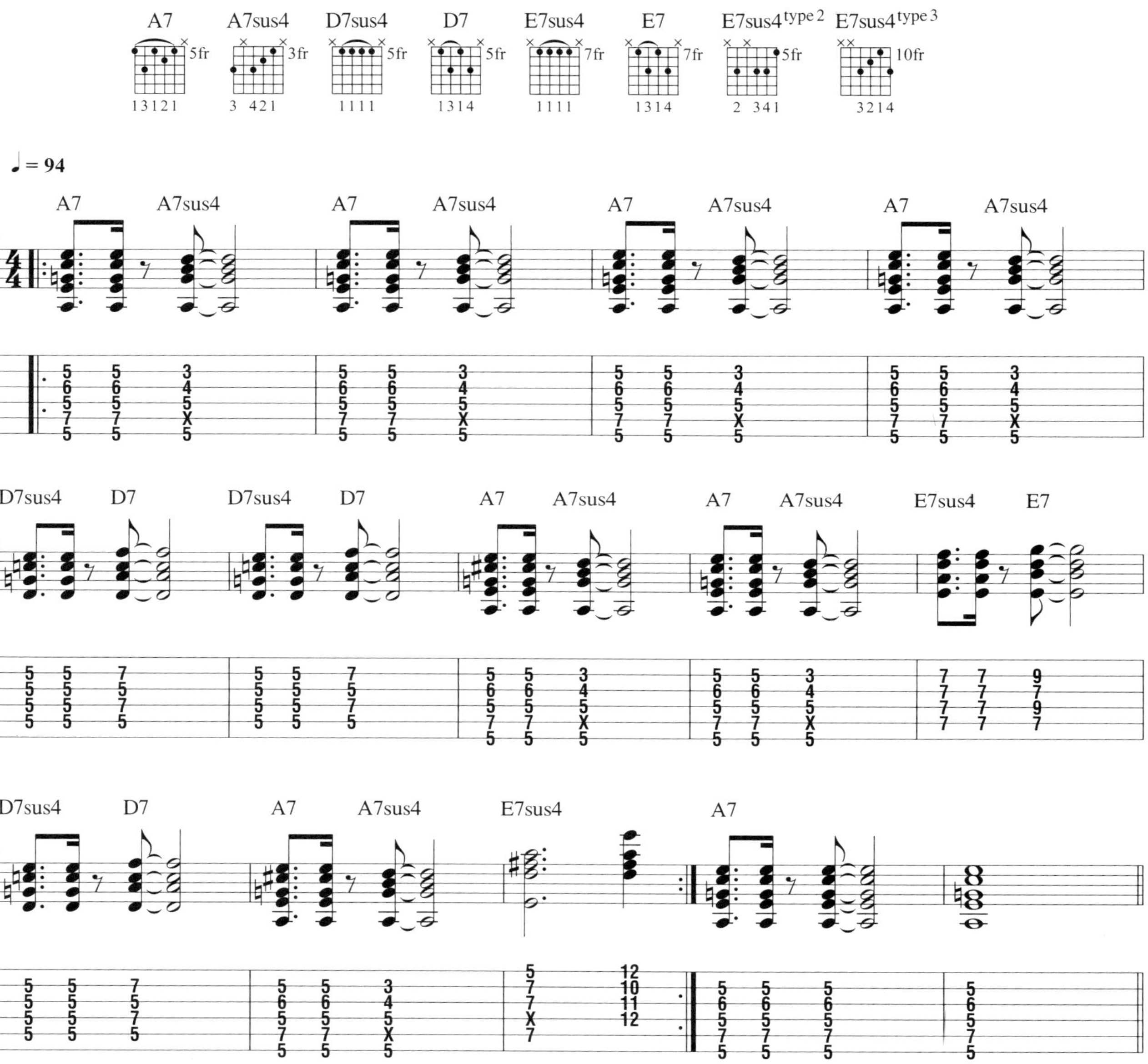

Another approach in the blues is to use triads over bass notes to create an interesting and less predictable sound. On the next page is an example that we used earlier in the book.

Example 30

This is played over a C bass note and works in place of C7. Let's analyze what's going on here: We have a Gm triad slinging up to an Am triad and back. Why do these triads work over a C bass to create a viable alternative to simply playing C7? Let's first explore where the chord C7 comes from. In any major key, when we harmonize it to four notes, we get four different types of 7th chords. In the key of C, we get the following: Cmaj7–Dm7–Em7–Fmaj7–G7–Am7–Bm7♭5. As you can see, we only get a plain dominant 7th chord built from the fifth note of the major scale. In this case, we want to understand which key C7 comes from. To do that, we need to figure out which major scale would have C as its fifth note. The answer to that is F—the C7 chord belongs to the key of F major.

Now let's explore which triads are formed from the key of F: F–Gm–Am–B♭–C–Dm–E°. As you can see, the Am and Gm triads from our original chord riff are contained within the key that C7 belongs to. By simply placing these two triads over a C bass, we created a viable alternative chord structure to simply strumming a C7 chord. With this in mind, let's look at all of those triads, keeping them on the same string set as our original riff:

C7 Chord Scale

Example 31

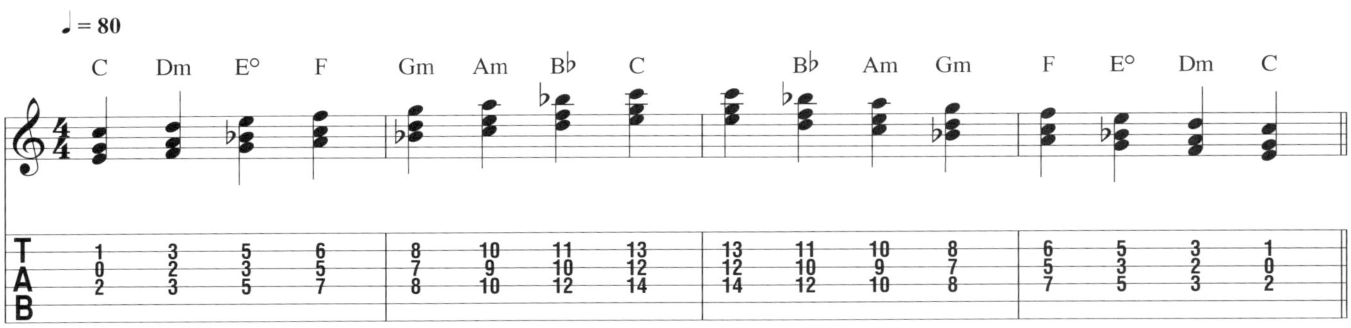

I started this from the lowest chord available on the neck. We start on a C triad and work our way through the harmonized F major scale. You will notice the Gm and Am triads from our original riff exist within these chords.

On the next page is a riff that incorporates some of the triads we listed. This is an example of a musical application of a theoretical idea. We could technically learn these examples with no theoretical knowledge, but as you can see, understanding where it came from can help us to come up with our own alternative.

C7 Alternative

Example 32

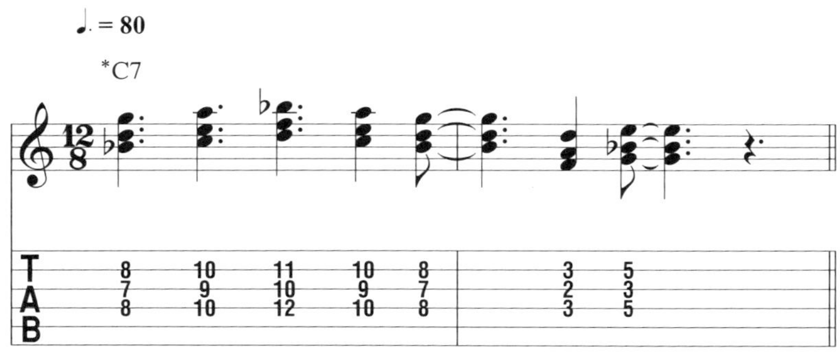

*Chord symbols reflect basic harmony.

So far, this example has been applied over a C7 chord. We would need to repeat the same process for the other chords in a blues. For example, in a C blues we have C7, F7, and G7. We've already figured out that C7 is from the key of F major. Which major key would F7 belong to? First, we need to figure out which major scale has F as its fifth note. That would be the key of B♭. If we harmonize the key of B♭ as triads we would get: B♭–Cm–Dm–E♭–F–Gm–A°. Now let's play those on the same string set as the C7 triads:

F7 Chord Scale

Example 33

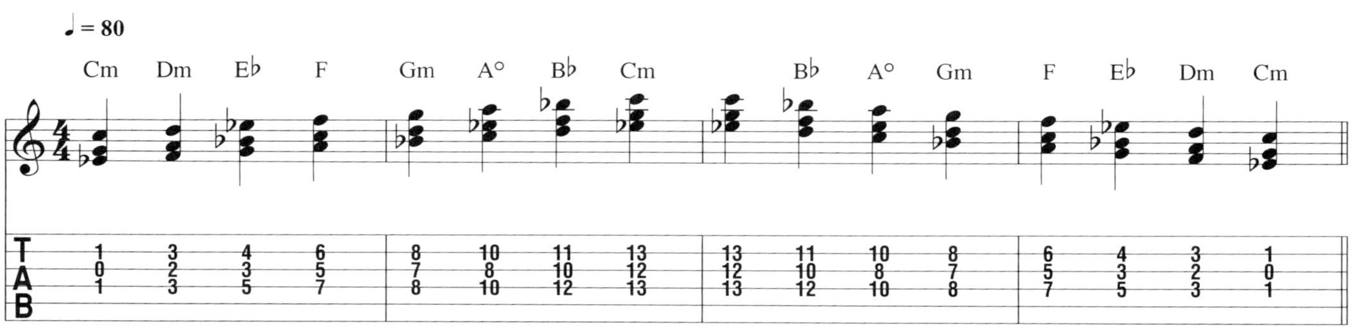

For the V chord in the C blues, we need the triads that would fit with G7. G7 is the V chord in the C major scale. Here is the C major scale harmonized as triads: C, Dm, Em, F, G, Am, B°. Here are the triads played in a scalar fashion over the fretboard:

G7 Chord Scale

Example 34

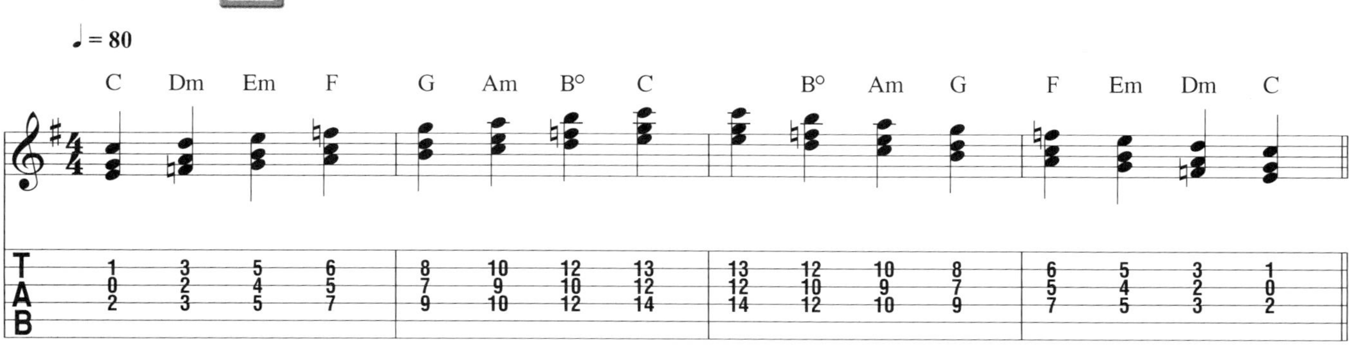

Now that we have figured out the triads that go with each chord in the C blues, we should experiment with them to create interesting pieces that explore the idea of mixing melody with chordal playing. This is a great thing to add into your improvising so that all your solos are not only single notes. It also makes you a more versatile accompanist.

You need to memorize all these shapes and keep the C blues chord progression in your mind at all times. If you do not play the relevant set of chords at the correct time, it will completely clash. For example, when C7 is playing in the blues, you should only be playing the C7 chord scale triads. Do not keep playing the C7 chord scale triads when the chord has changed to F7 or G7. It is also imperative that you memorize the blues chord progression. If you are unsure of which chord is coming next in the progression, then you are not ready. I used to spend hours simply speaking the chord progression of the blues out loud, making a concerted effort to have it completely memorized so that there was never any doubt in my mind about what was coming next. I recommend you practice this even without the guitar in your hand. Once you have it memorized, you will be able to better concentrate on the music.

Now let's take a look at these chord scale triads practically applied to a blues chord progression. Take your time learning this one:

Blues Chord Solo

Example 35

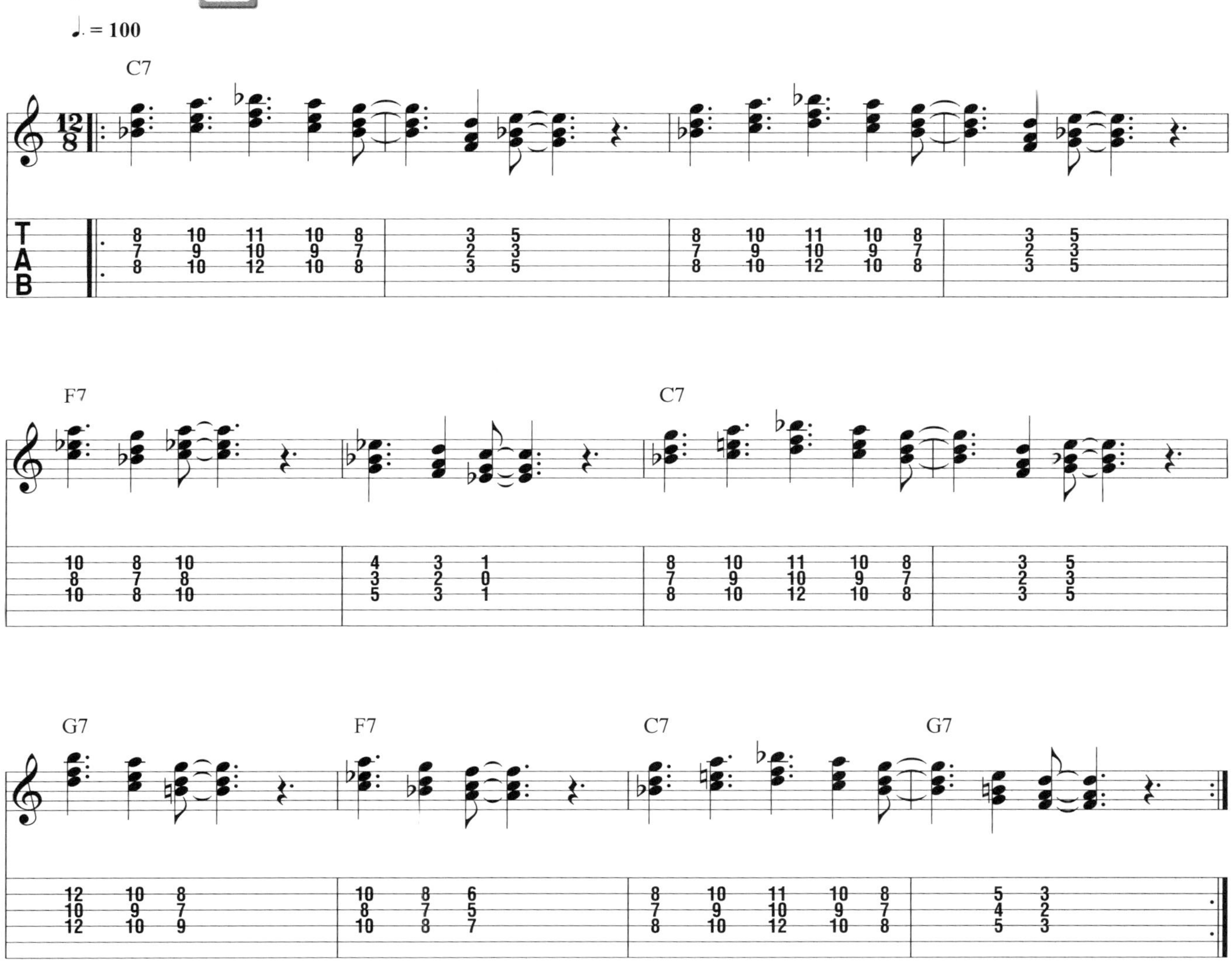

Now let's look at another blues chord example, this time in E (be sure to slightly mute the low E and A strings throughout):

Chord Riff Blues

Example 36

In the previous example, we basically took the same approach with triads. Some of these are on different string sets. For example, this occurs with the E7. These triads are from the key of A major (from which E7 derives) and the triads occur on strings A, D, and G. It is good to know your triad shapes on different string sets so you can be versatile when playing these riffs. Here are the triad shapes that fit over E7:

E7 Chord Scale

Example 37

Once you are familiar enough with any scale along the neck, you can take any random notes from the scale and move them around, and they don't have to be your traditional triads. For example, here is the E Mixolydian scale (fifth mode of the A major scale):

E Mixolydian

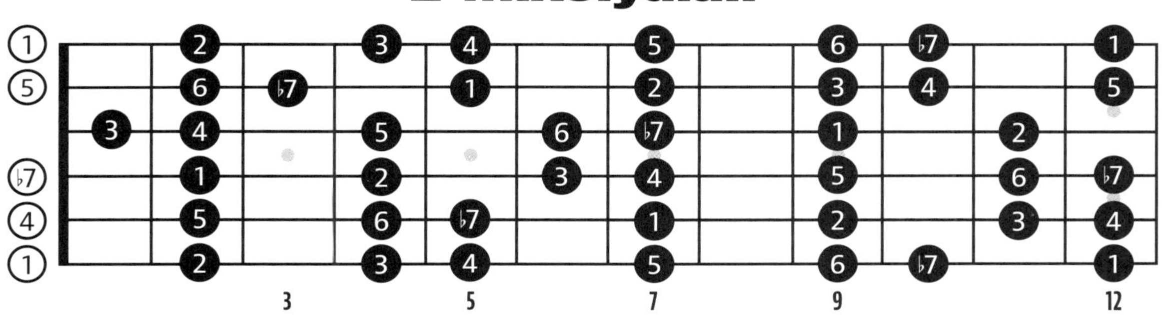

The diagram below is another way to look at the previous C7, F7, and G7 chord scales. You can clearly see the scale covering the entire fretboard, and that I have highlighted the triads with a line connecting each one. It is important to understand that we can see these triads different ways, intervalically. We can see them from their own roots as the familiar triads that we know and love, but we also see them in the context of the scale they are pulled from, which gives them different intervals in relation to the root of the scale. For example, we might see a Dm triad, but in relation to the root of the scale, it may be functioning with completely different intervals. This is the reason I have the intervals labeled within the scale so you can see how each triad is functioning.

C Mixolydian

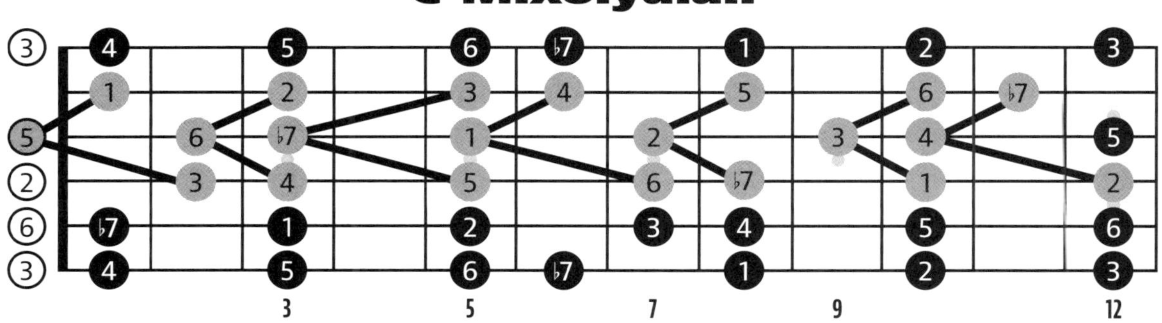

Right here, we can see these triads from low to high as C–Dm–E°–F–Gm–Am–B♭. The C is functioning intervallically as a C triad within the context of C Mixolydian, since C is the root of that scale. However, Dm is not. What would be the root of the Dm (D) is functioning as the 2nd degree of C Mixolydian. The Dm triad itself contains the 2nd, 4th, and 6th degrees of the scale. That makes it a *suspended* sounding chord. It's good to experiment with each triad see how each one sounds over a C root. Some are more like passing chords that need to lead somewhere, whereas some sound stable and resolved.

I also encourage you to come up with your own chord shapes—the sky is the limit. As long as the notes are contained within the scale, they are perfectly consonant sounds.

Next, let's take a look at the chords from F Mixolydian. From left to right, the F Mixolydian chords are: Cm–Dm–E♭–F–Gm–A°–B♭.

F Mixolydian

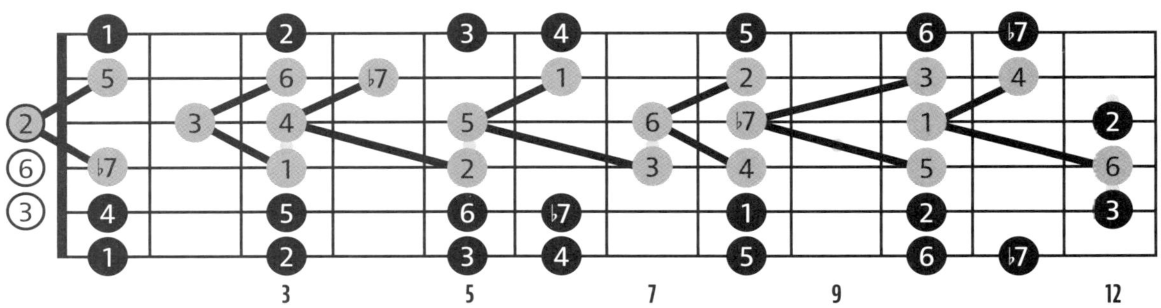

It's interesting to compare the chords to the other scales. For example, in C Mixolydian we had a C major triad, but in F Mixolydian, it's C minor. These small changes can be great things to emphasize while we improvise.

Here are the triads from left to right inside G Mixolydian: C–Dm–Em–F–G–Am–B°.

G Mixolydian

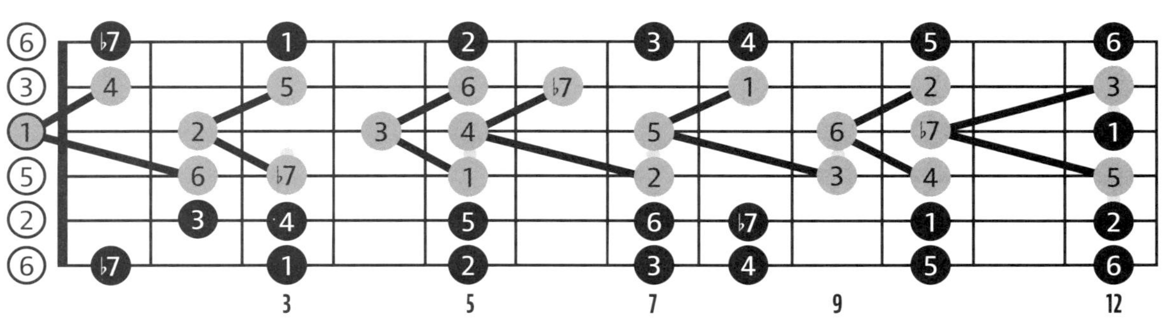

You can see G Mixolydian has the first two triads in common with C Mixolydian, but the third one is Em (in G Mixolydian), whereas it's E° in C Mixolydian. It's great to notice and play on these differences as the blues chord progression goes by.

Now let's look at playing the triads for C7, F7, and G7 on different string sets. I recommend that you ultimately learn them on all string sets and in different inversions. Here are those same triads but on strings 3, 2, and 1:

C Mixolydian

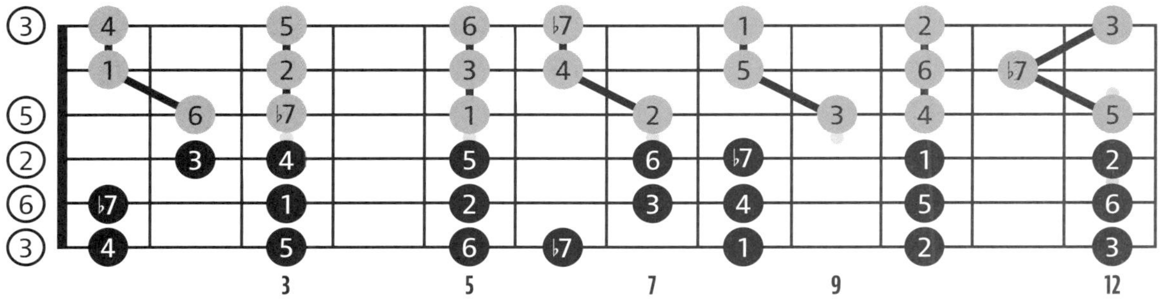

F Mixolydian

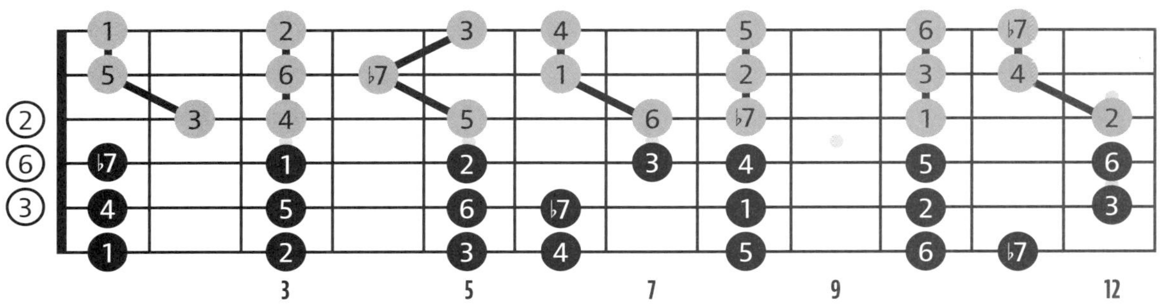

G Mixolydian

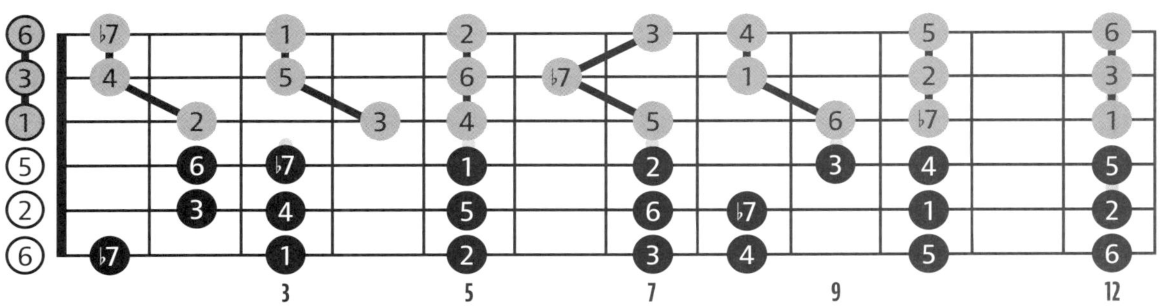

Here is another inversion example on strings 3, 2, and 1:

C Mixolydian

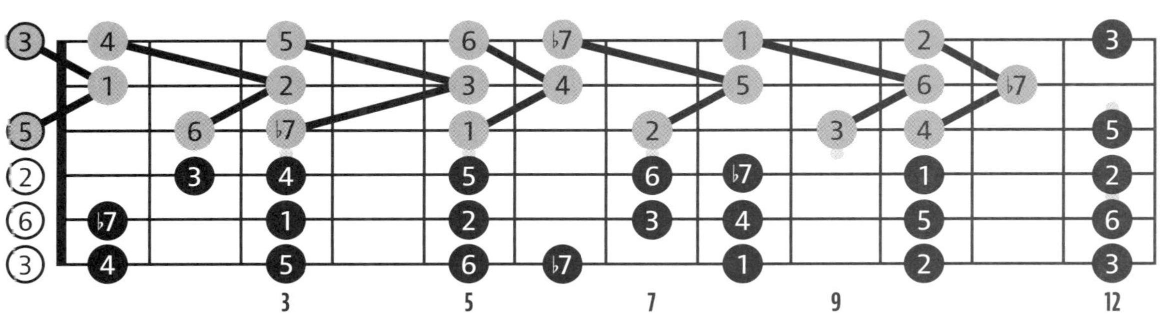

Here is a musical example that I created using the original 4, 3, and 2 string sets in combination with these new 3, 2, and 1 string sets:

String Combination Blues

Example 38

2 Double Stops

Now that we have spent time learning chord scales, triads, and extended chords, I would like to talk about *double stops*. Double stops are another great technique to add to your solos. A double stop is simply two notes played together simultaneously. From any scale, we can take any two notes and play them together. This goes for full seven-note scales as well as pentatonic scales. In a seven-note scale, we can have 2nds, 3rds, 4ths, 5ths, 6ths, 7ths, octaves, and even compound intervals like 9ths and 10ths. Each one has its own unique sound. Let's first explore 3rds, as they are arguably the most used and melodic double stops. Let's take a look:

C Mixolydian

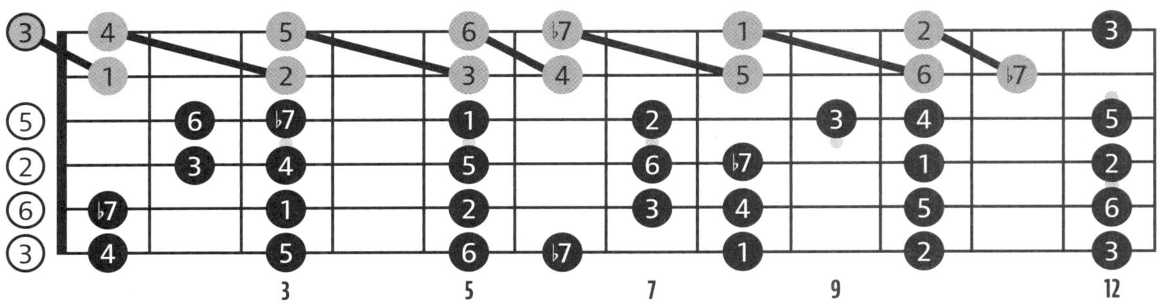

Here, we are playing the 3rds on strings 2 and 1 in C Mixolydian, meaning that these 3rds would work perfectly over the C7 chord in a C blues. It is important to learn our 3rds on all string sets, as this allows us to freely improvise no matter what string sets we are on. It is also important to learn the 3rds for all the chords in the blues. So in our C blues, we would need to learn the 3rds within C7, F7, and G7.

Let's take a look at all the 3rds for C7 on all the string sets:

C Mixolydian 3rds

Example 39

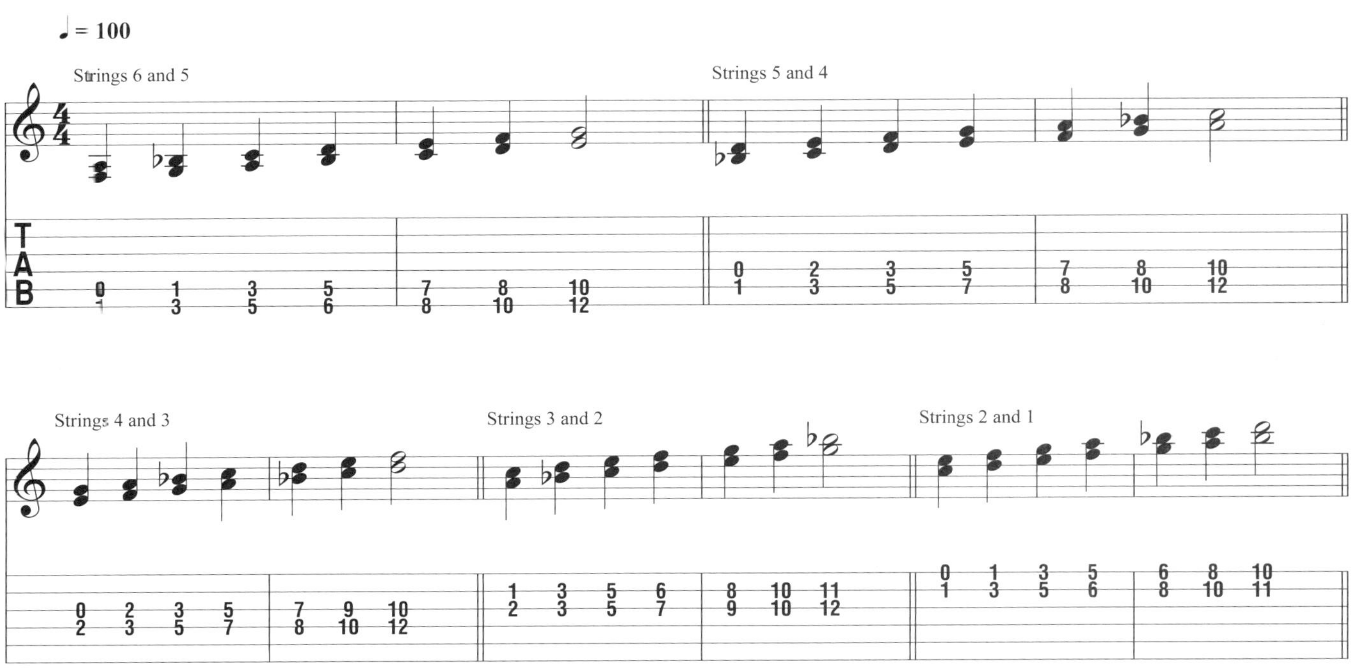

These 3rds are all started from the lowest place found on each string set. It's important to understand where the root notes are in each one. The root will appear on the lower and upper strings at different points within each set. It is essential that you know where your notes are located on the neck of the guitar to really be in control. It's worth taking the time to learn those so you are properly oriented.

Now that we have the 3rds for C7, we should next learn the 3rds for F7 and G7 to have a complete overview of the fretboard. Here is the neck chart to see the 3rds in F Mixolydian on the first two strings in context:

F Mixolydian

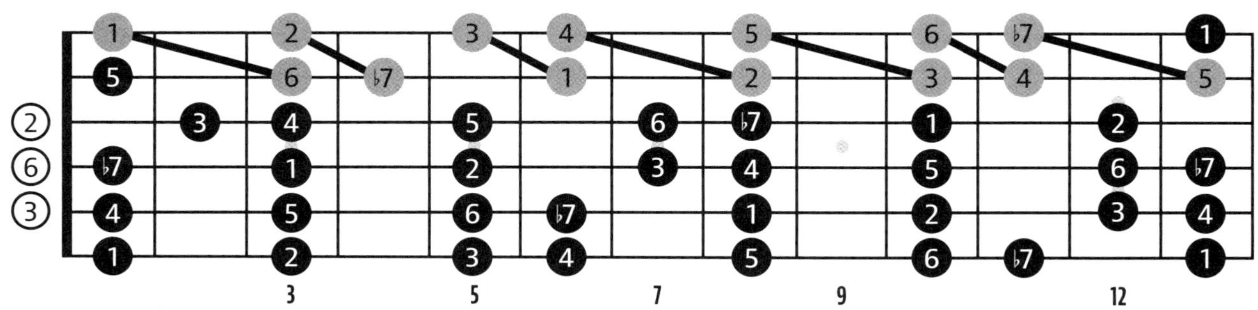

F Mixolydian 3rds

Example 40

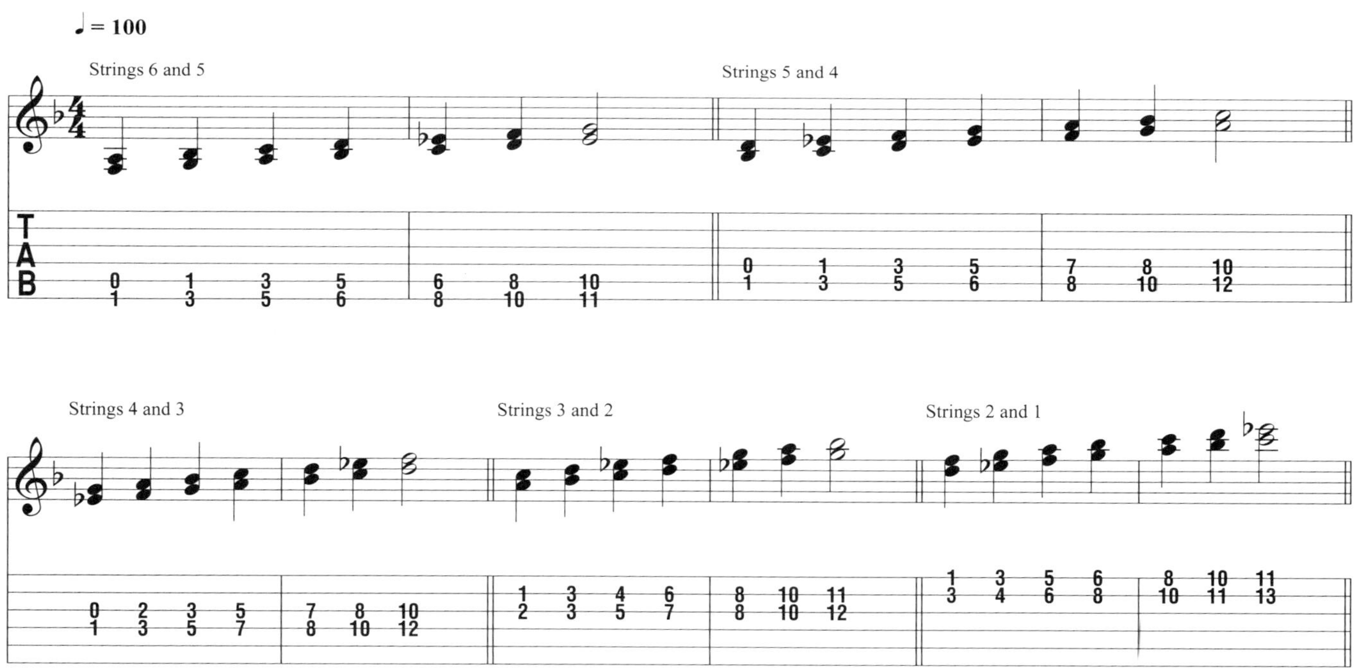

Here is the same kind of chart to visualize the 3rds in G Mixolydian on strings 2 and 1:

G Mixolydian

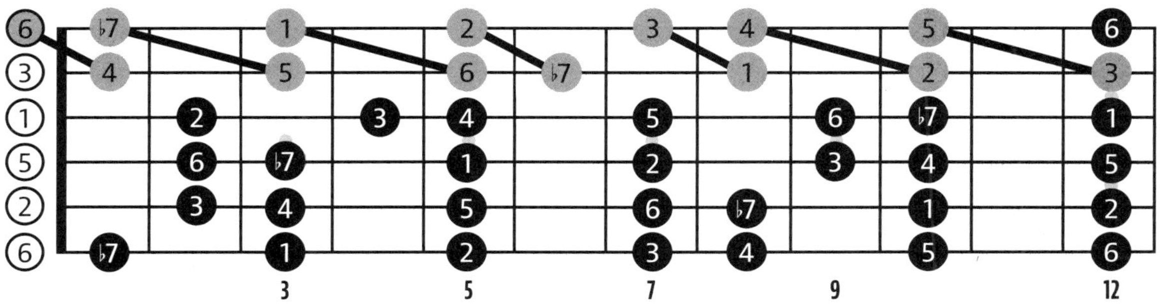

G Mixolydian 3rds

Example 41

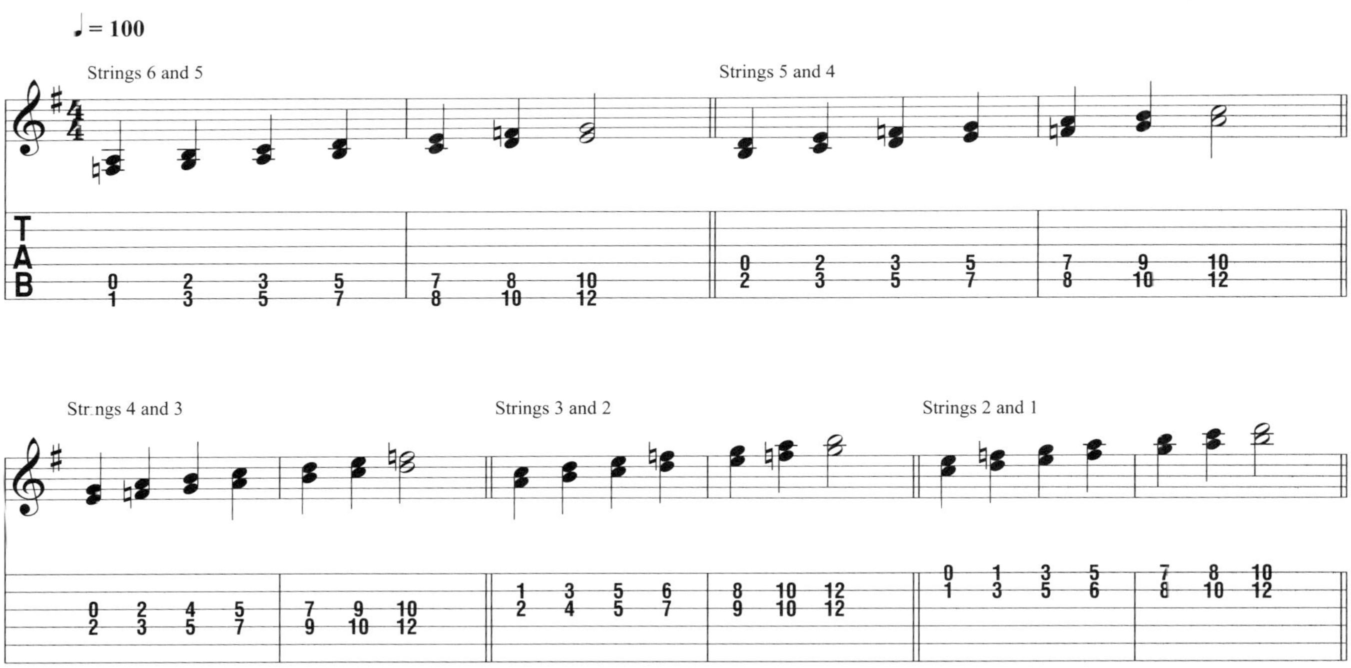

On the next page is an example combining 3rds for each chord over a blues progression in C. In addition to practicing these examples, please take the time to learn all the 3rds so that you can understand what is going on musically. This will allow you to create your own exercises.

Blues 3rds

Example 42

Now let's talk about introducing chromaticism (connecting notes by half steps) between the 3rds. If we have two of the same shape a whole step apart (two frets), we can connect them chromatically. For example, here are descending 3rds in C Mixolydian. First, we see two of the narrower shape two frets apart, followed by two of the wider shape two frets apart:

Example 43

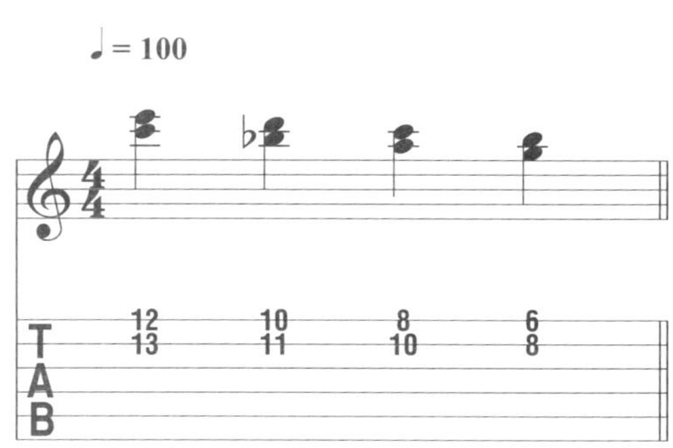

We can link these shapes with a chromatic version of the same shape in between. For example, here are the two narrow double stops connected chromatically:

Example 44

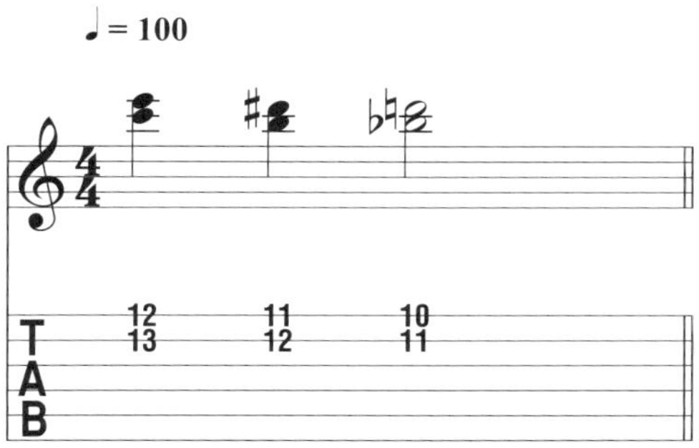

The first and third beats are the 3rds coming from C Mixolydian, but the second beat is a chromatic passing 3rd. Let's do the same for the wider shape:

Example 45

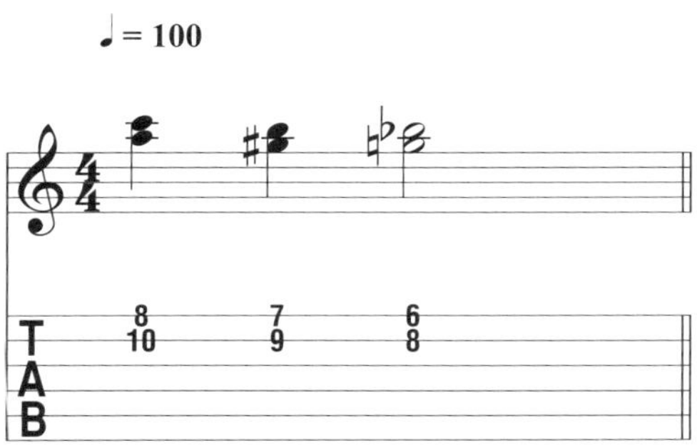

With this knowledge, we can add these chromatic 3rds into the mix to create some cool and tense colors that lend themselves to the blues sound.

Here is a lick over C7 using 3rds from C Mixolydian along with chromatics:

Example 46

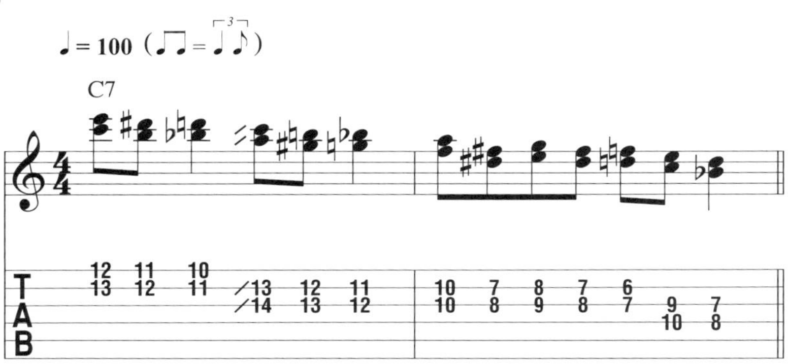

This lick utilizes the chromatic 3rds in a way that adds a lot of interest to a simple 3rds lick. Experiment with your own variations.

Here's a chromatic 3rds lick over F7:

Example 47

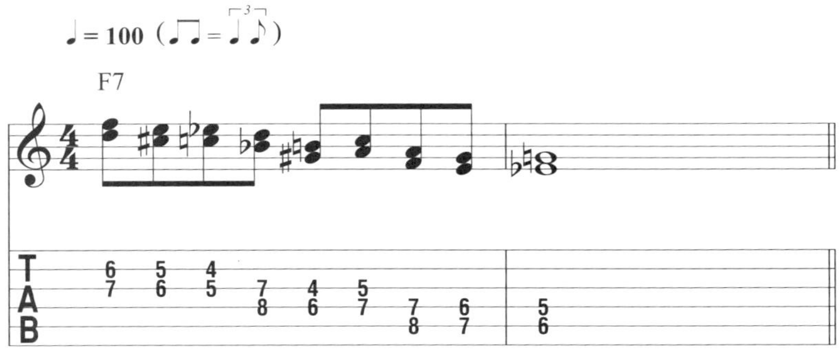

Let's look at another lick over G7:

Example 48

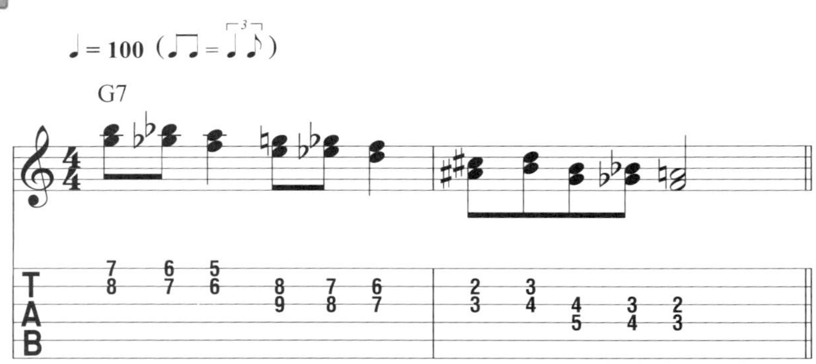

With each of these licks, take the time to learn where the chromatic 3rds are to gain an understanding of how the tension really adds something to the phrase.

We don't always have to start on an "inside" 3rd either. This means we can technically start on a chromatic 3rd to give us a feeling of leading into the 3rd from below. The above example can work also if done with confidence. Here is an example of chromatic 3rds leading into the more resolved, "inside" 3rds:

Example 49

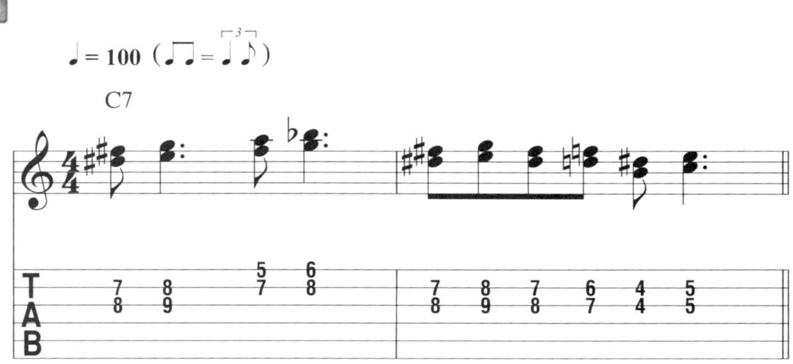

Now let's look at a blues example containing these same concepts:

Chromatic 3rds Blues

Example 50

These intervals don't always have to be played at the same time. We can also separate them as individual notes. Let's take a look at an example:

Example 51

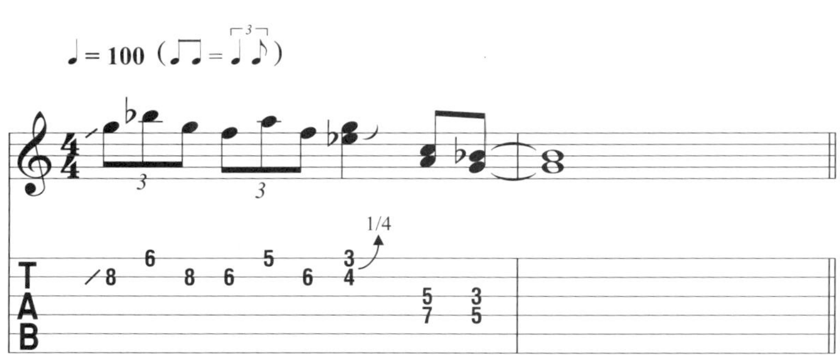

An interesting idea occurs on beat 3 where we play a 3rd with the lower note a half step lower than where it would normally be. Then, bend that lower note up to reach the desired note (which would usually be the fifth fret and not the fourth fret). This creates a tension which is quite synonymous with the blues.

Now let's take a look at 6th intervals. These are also very popular in a blues context. A 6th means, if we count up a full seven-note scale from a note (counting the starting note as 1) up 6, then we get a 6th interval. Because 6ths are further away than 3rds, they usually end up being played by skipping over a string. Because of this, you either need to mute the string in between or you have to use your pick in combination with a finger.

Let's take a look at 6th intervals over a C7:

C Mixolydian

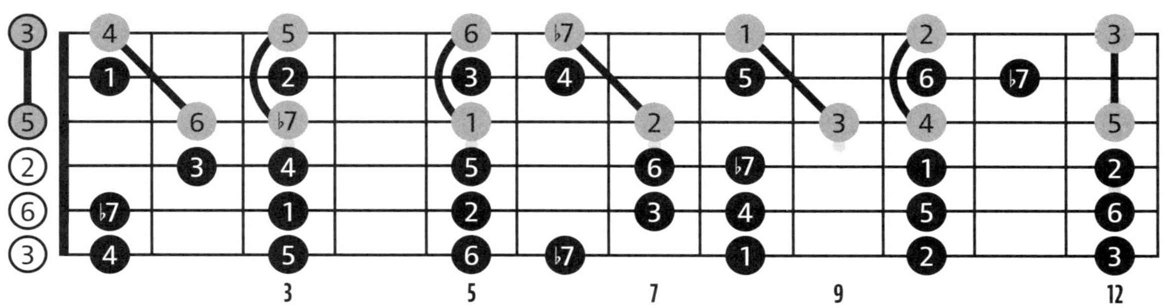

As you can see, just like with 3rds, there are two types of shapes: a narrower one and a wider one. What I am calling the narrower shape has its notes on the same fret and the wider one has the other note a fret lower. Let's look at these in tab form and on every string set:

C Mixolydian 6ths

Example 52

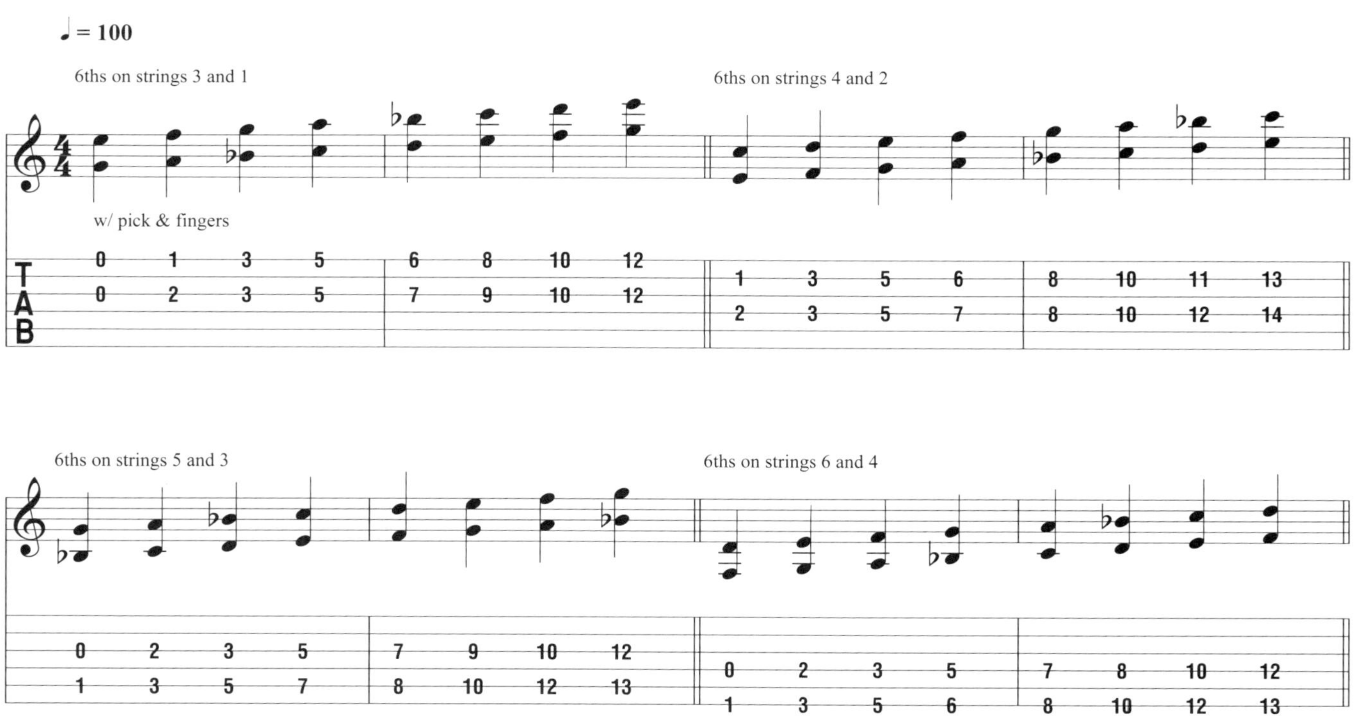

All of these 6th intervals will work over the C7 in our blues chord progression. Here is a typical blues lick in C7 using 6th intervals with some chromatic passing 6ths:

Example 53

This is an example of a 6ths lick where we combine separating the 6ths and playing them simultaneously. It also contains a chromatic 6th on the 11th fret on the G and E strings. Now let's learn the 6ths in F Mixolydian to fit over our F7 Chord, followed by 6ths on every string set:

F Mixolydian

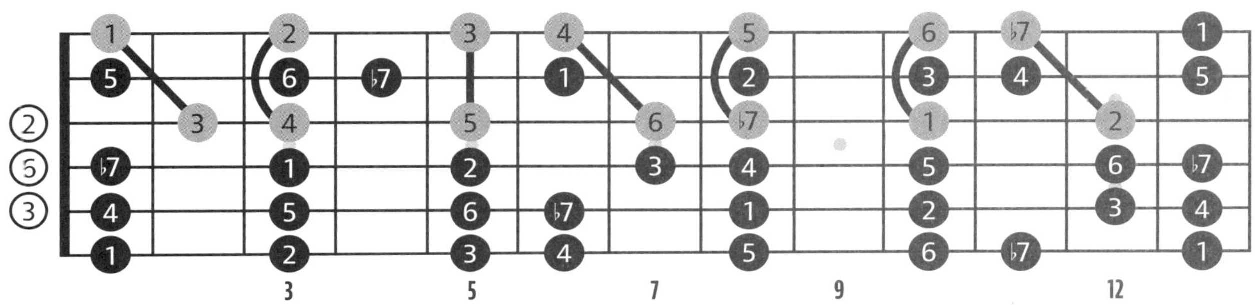

F Mixolydian 6ths

Example 54

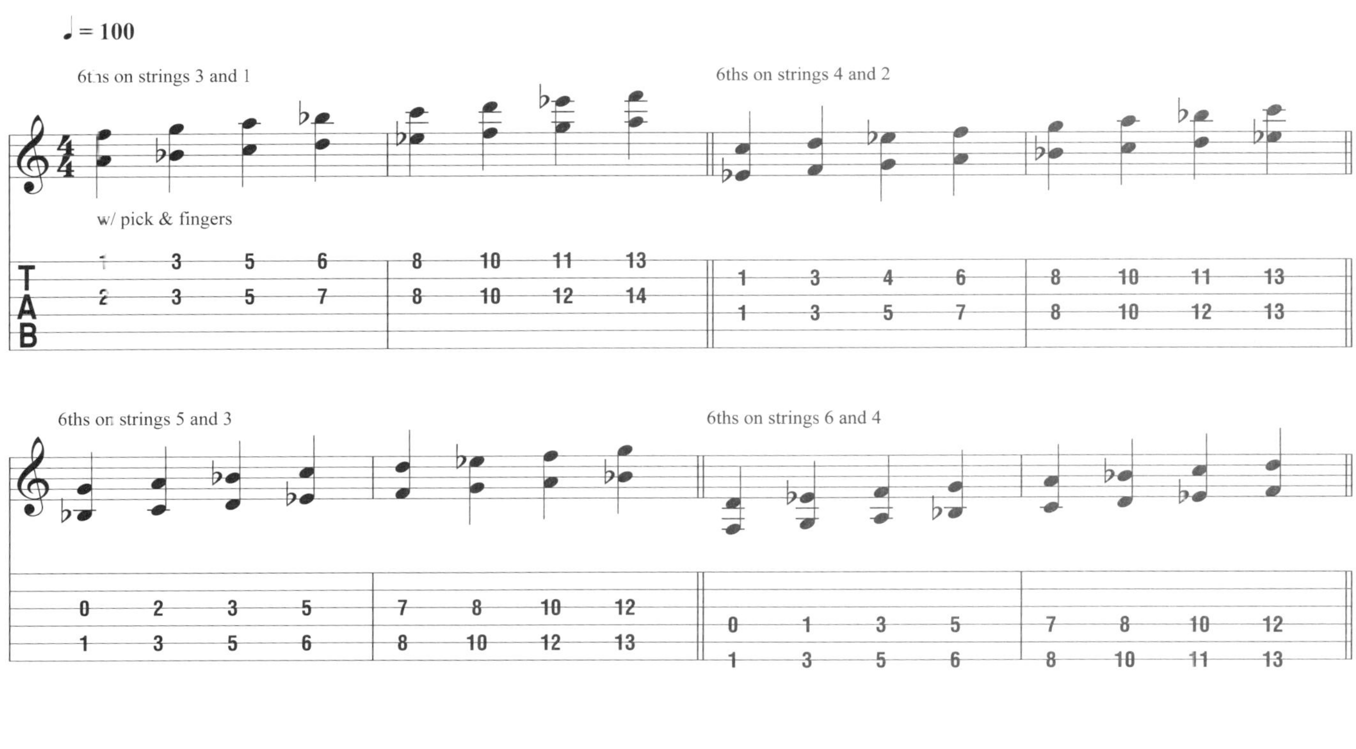

And now let's look at 6ths in G7:

G Mixolydian

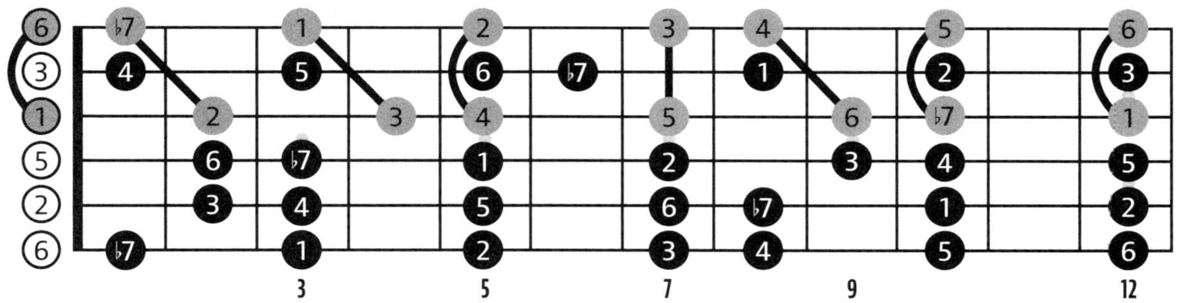

Now let's learn the G7 Mixolydian 6ths on every string set:

G Mixolydian 6ths

Example 55

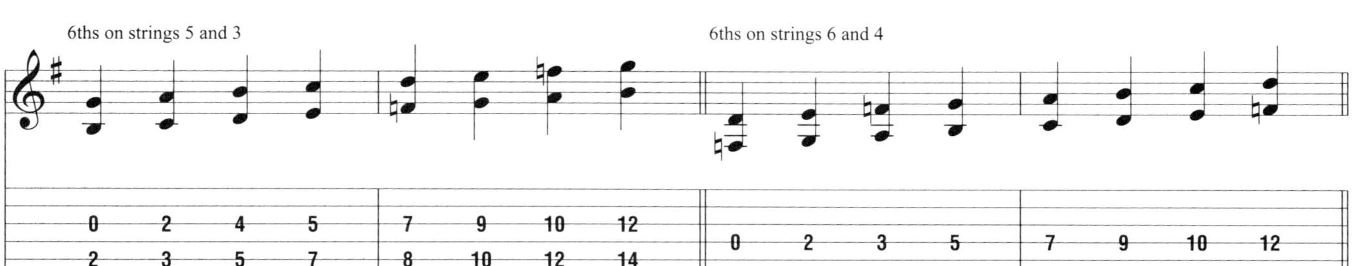

Now let's learn an example that uses the 6th intervals in a blues. I will also throw in some chromatic passing 6ths:

Chromatic 6ths Blues

Example 56

This is a great example of the 6th intervals being used in a blues context and following each chord individually as it changes. Pay attention to where the chromatic 6ths are and memorize this example.

Of course, we can combine approaches so that we have 6ths and 3rds used together. Let's take a look at this example which combines both approaches with some chromaticism thrown in for good measure:

Chromatic 6ths and 3rds Blues

Example 57

Continuing on from the last example, let's throw triads into the mix for a varied approach:

Full Combination: 3rds, 6ths, and Triads

Example 58

That example contained 6ths, 3rds, triads, and chromaticism. Experiment by coming up with your own, and be sure to practice them over different keys.

3 Single-Note Soloing Approaches

Using the Minor Pentatonic Scale

When soloing in the blues, the most common approach that we take when we first learn to solo is with the minor pentatonic scale. This is a great approach and we still use it even as we get more advanced. I aim to show you some extra approaches we can add in to this already solid approach for soloing. One of the most common things I notice with guitar players who have just learned their minor pentatonic scale is that they don't really react to the chord changes in the blues and simply play the same licks regardless of when the chords change. This leads to a solo that can sound directionless and lacking in melody.

First of all, I want to outline to you the concept of the meaning of each note changing when the chord changes. For example, if we are doing a blues in the key of A, the chords are A7, D7, and E7. Let's focus on one note in our A minor pentatonic scale, let's say A. This note will change meaning with regards to the chord it's played over. When played over A7, the note A functions as the root. When the chord changes to D7, the A note becomes the 5th in relation to the D7 chord. Finally, when played over the E7, the A note becomes the 4th (11th) of that chord. The A note sounds at rest over the A7 and D7 chords because it becomes a chord tone. But over the E7, the A note does not sound very at rest, as the 4th clashes with the 3rd of the chord (G♯). Let me illustrate this by showing you diagrams of the A minor pentatonic as it relates intervallically to each chord in an A blues:

A Minor Pentatonic over A7

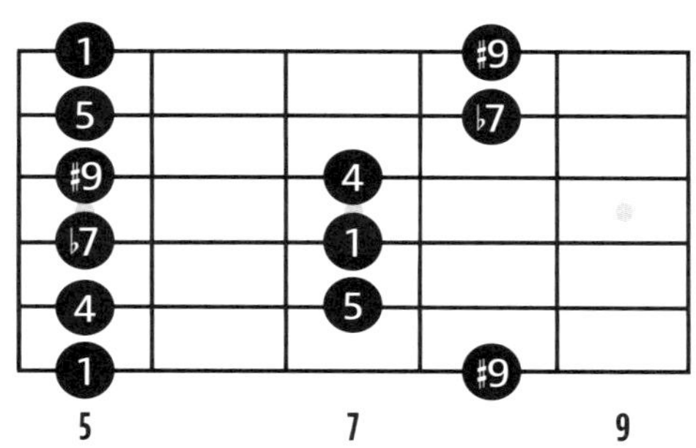

A Minor Pentatonic over D7

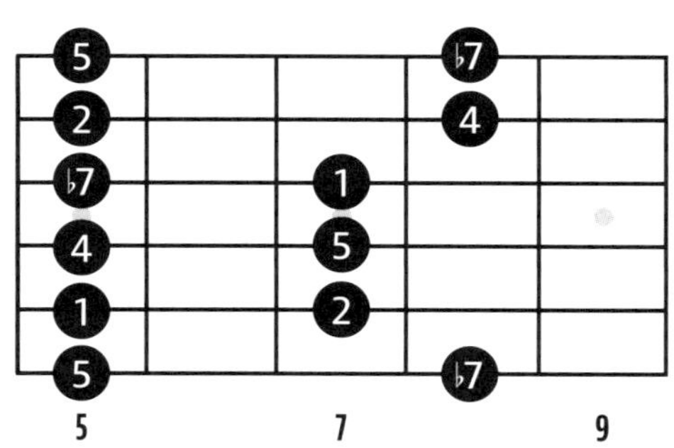

A Minor Pentatonic over E7

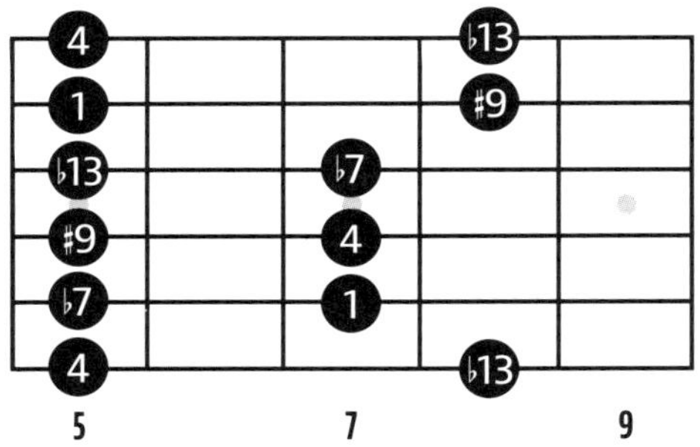

As you can see, the intervals of those same A minor pentatonic notes change depending on which of the three chords they are played over. We are playing them over dominant 7th chords, which contain the following intervals: 1–3–5–♭7.

When playing the minor pentatonic notes over the A7, we have the root, the ♭3 (which we can bend up a half step to become the 3rd), the 5th, and the ♭7. So, almost all the notes of the A7 chord are contained within the scale. We need to learn where these strong notes are. Here is an outline of all the strong notes held when playing them over the A7:

Example 59

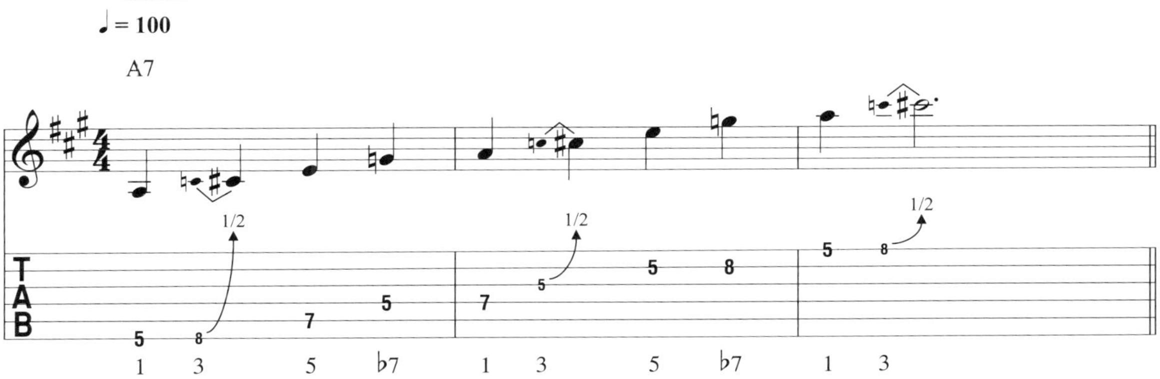

This doesn't mean that we can't or shouldn't play the other notes, it simply means that we see the other notes as stepping stones to get to the strong ones. The notes highlighted are simply the strong notes when played over the A7 chord. It's important to understand that the intervals listed underneath are the target intervals when there is a bend symbol.

Now let's consider the A minor pentatonic over D7. The A minor pentatonic contains the D root, the 2nd (which can be bent up a whole step to become a 3rd), the 5th, and the ♭7. It's not always practical to bend up the 9th to the 3rd, particularly on the B string which would require a position change, but it's good to know where it is. Let's take a look at that:

Example 60

It's really important to be aware of where these notes sit, and be sure to accentuate the strong notes in accordance to the chord that you are playing over. This seems like a lot to think about initially, but it will make your playing much stronger. Now let's look at A minor pentatonic when played over the E7 chord. It contains the E root, the ♭3 (which can be bent up a half step to reach the 3rd), the 5th (bending up from the 4th, but not always practical), and the ♭7. Here is that example:

Example 61

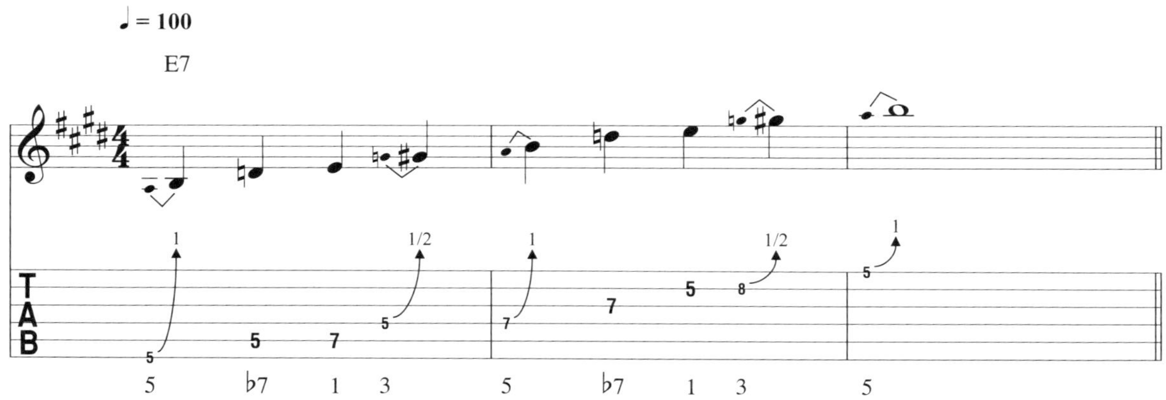

Armed with this knowledge, let's look at this 12-bar blues solo in A that uses only the A minor pentatonic scale, but we are really honing in on each individual chord as it is presented within the progression:

Smarty Pants Blues

Example 62

This highlights why the A minor pentatonic and blues scales are so popular when starting out in the blues. The notes mostly work with all three chords, but don't really fit any one of the chords perfectly, especially the E7. Many players would shift to an E minor pentatonic, bending out its minor 3rd (G) to become the major 3rd (G♯). You can even play the minor pentatonic scale of each chord, but the A minor pentatonic works very well on both the A7 and D7. With the focus of this book being on advancing the blues, let's take a close look at what the good notes really are for each chord.

Using Arpeggios

When playing over a chord, it is important to know the arpeggio of that chord so we truly know where the strongest notes are. Earlier in the book, we touched on the guide tones (the 3rd and 7th of each chord). These are great, but let's dive in a little deeper. If we play over a dominant 7th chord, the chord tones are: 1–3–5–♭7. Let's learn these as shapes on the fretboard (D7 and E7 appear on the next page):

A7 Arpeggio

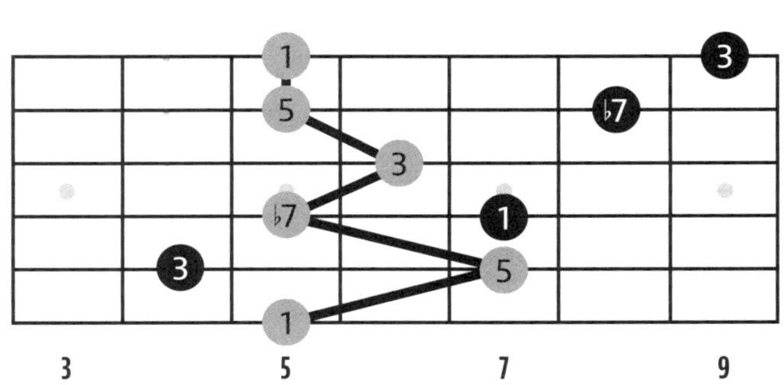

D7 Arpeggio

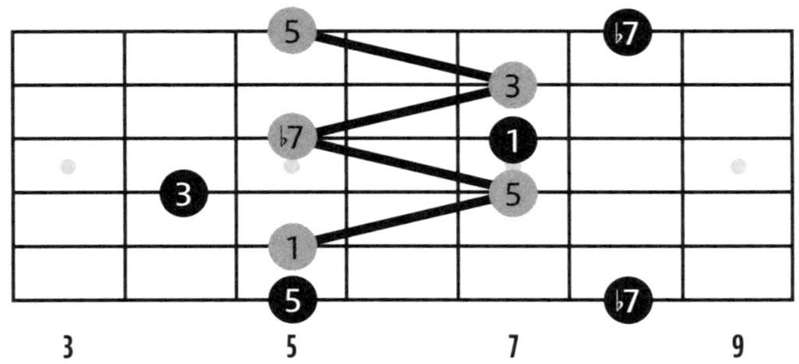

E7 Arpeggio

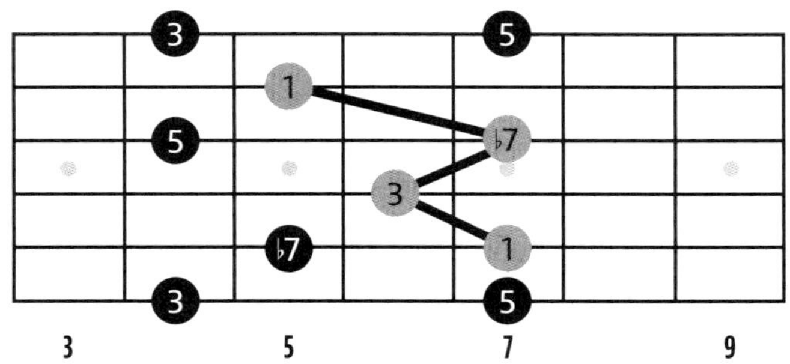

These three shapes are all placed around the same fret region so that the hand doesn't have to shift positions. Rather than taking one shape and moving it along the fretboard, we learn these three shapes to make it more ergonomic. It is really important that you not only learn where the roots are (for changing keys), but also understand where the related chord shapes lie. I have connected the notes of the chord shapes with a line. Learn the root, the chord shape, and then the arpeggio, from lowest to highest note.

Once you have learned these shapes, practice linking them together in the simplest of ways through a blues chord progression.

Connecting the Arpeggios

Example 63

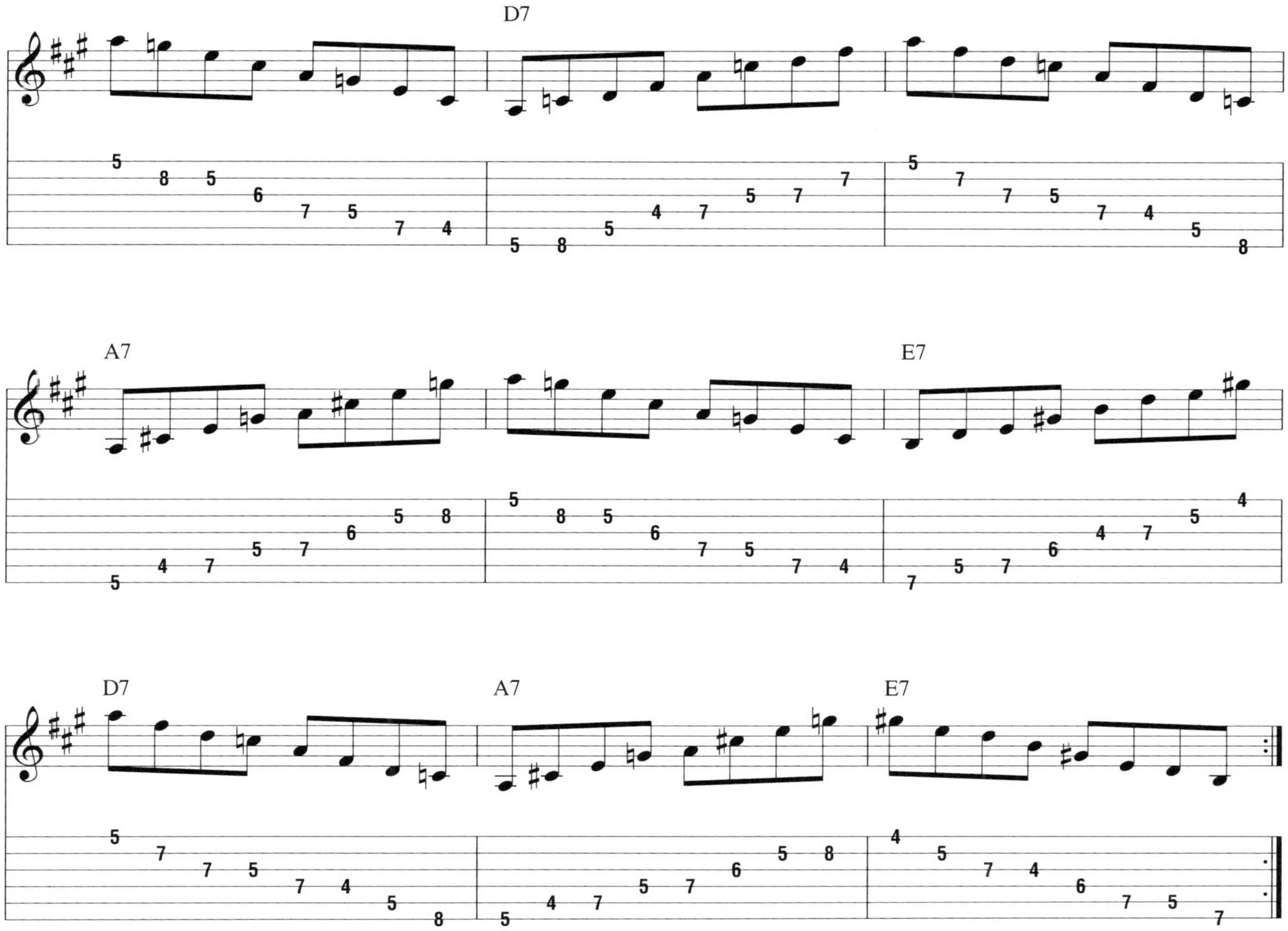

This is a basic way that we can practice connecting the arpeggios. However, it tends to sound like an exercise (albeit an important one for visualization purposes). Let's explore some ways we can make these arpeggios sound a little more musical.

Example 64 appears on the next page to allow for easier reading.

Arpeggio Blues Solo

Example 64

I introduced the quick change in this blues example. As you can hear, this is already a lot more musical than simply running the arpeggios up and down. It can sound somewhat stiff to only stick to the notes in the arpeggio, though. This is where chromatic passing tones come in, as well as combining the arpeggios with pentatonic scales.

Any note in the arpeggio can be led into with a chromatic note from beneath (and above, technically). This can also be done using a scale note below or above (the associated Mixolydian scale, in this case). Let's focus on the chromatic notes for a second. The 3rd is an especially good note to lead into from the chromatic below. The chromatic note below the 3rd is considered the ♭3rd (♯9), which is prevalent in the minor pentatonic scale that we explored previously. Let's take a look at adding this into the mix of the arpeggios:

A7 Arpeggio with Added ♯9

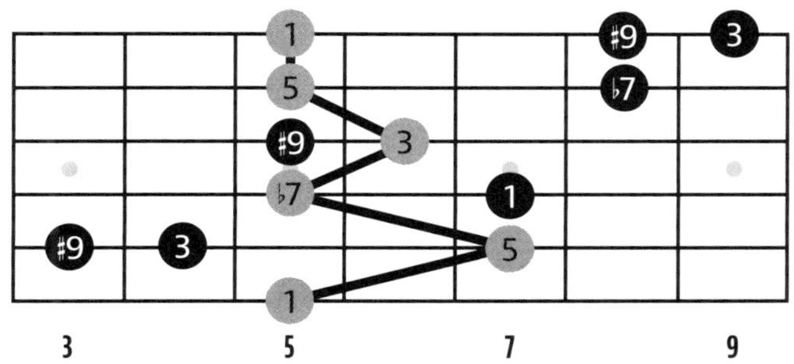

D7 Arpeggio with Added ♯9

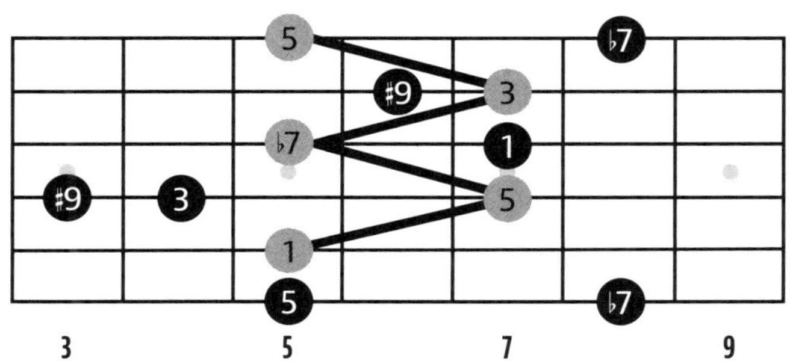

E7 Arpeggio with Added ♯9

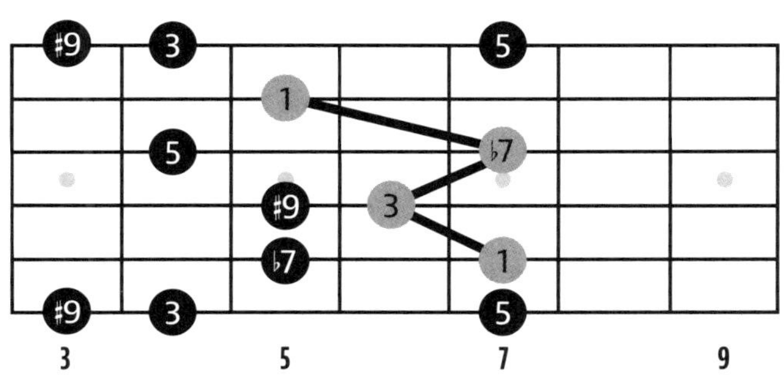

Rather than seeing these as entirely new shapes, simply see them as the same shapes we've been studying, but with a chromatic note below each 3rd. It is important that you think of the intervals as you play these arpeggios and get used to the sound of each one.

On the next page, let's look at a blues example using this chromatic approach concept with the 7th arpeggios and mixing in some of the minor pentatonic scales that we've learned so far.

Arpeggios with Chromaticism

Example 65

Make sure you learn this piece well and take mental note of which notes are in the arpeggio (chord tones) and which are the chromatic notes. Try to apply this concept into your improvisations.

Combining Scales and Arpeggios

Now I want to talk about adding notes to the dominant arpeggios to turn them into pentatonic scales. Remember, these 7th arpeggios contain four notes. That's just one note away from being a pentatonic scale. One really cool option that I will call dominant pentatonic is where we simply add the 2nd to the arpeggio. Let's take a look:

A7 Dominant Pentatonic

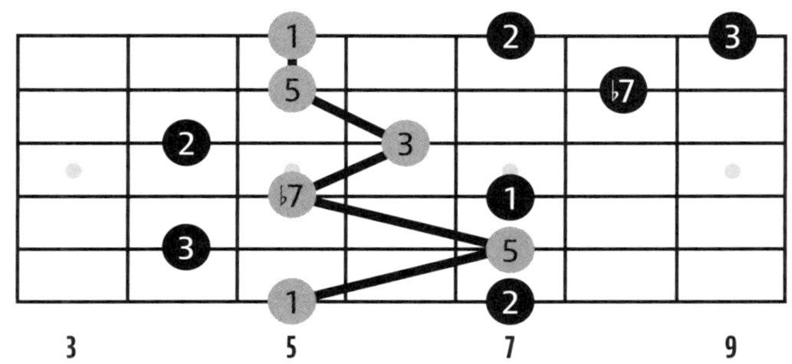

D7 Dominant Pentatonic

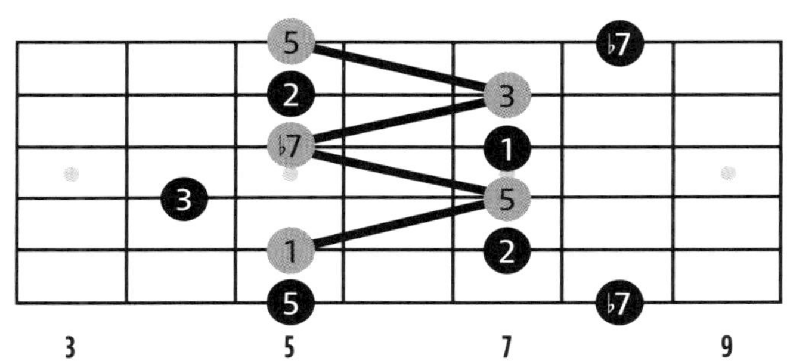

E7 Dominant Pentatonic

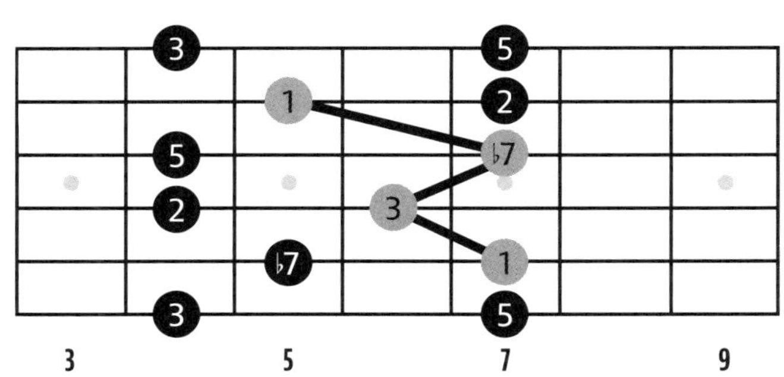

These pentatonics add a refreshing sound to the blues, and they get us away from the standard pentatonic scale we might be most familiar with. Let's add some of these ideas into a blues solo, located on the next page.

Creative Pentatonics

Example 66

This solo gives us an insight into some of the cool things we can experiment with in a blues context, and this really gets us thinking outside of the usual tried and tested licks.

As far as pentatonics go, we haven't focused on the major pentatonic scale yet. This scale is very sweet sounding and not particularly bluesy when used on its own. We generally use it alongside the minor pentatonic and weave between the two. The intervallic structure of the major pentatonic scale is: 1–2–3–5–6. If we consider that the Mixolydian scale is 1–2–3–4–5–6–♭7, we can see that the major pentatonic scale simply leaves out the 4 and ♭7.

Here is the major pentatonic scale built around chords from an A blues progression:

A Major Pentatonic

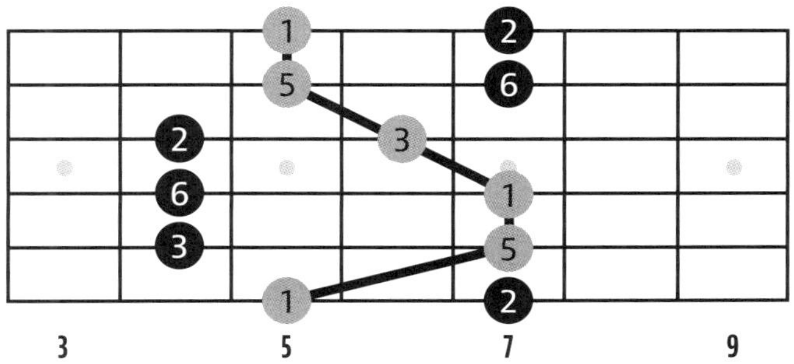

D Major Pentatonic

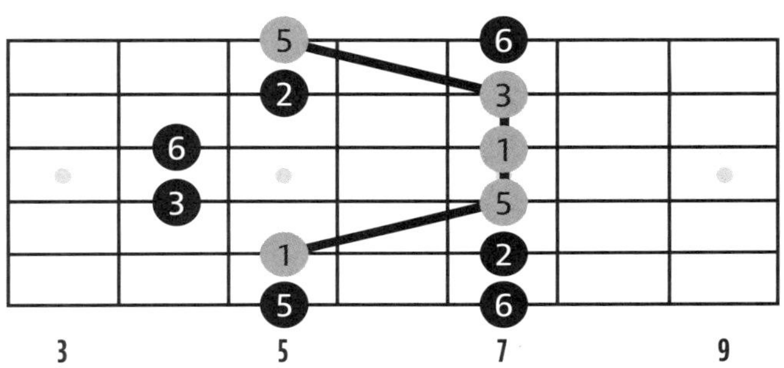

E Major Pentatonic

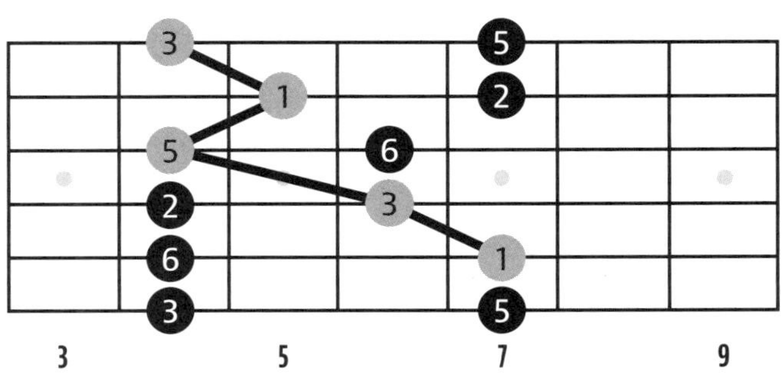

The major pentatonic scale is very similar to the dominant pentatonic scale we just learned. If we simply raise the 6th by one fret, it becomes a ♭7, making the scale identical to the dominant pentatonic. I like to take a leaf out of Peter Green's guitar playing in "The Stumble," which he performed in John Mayall and the Bluesbreakers. In bar 1 of that piece, he plays an A major pentatonic scale over an A chord, but then, he bends the 6th up a half step to become the ♭7. This is a really cool effect which I use quite a lot when playing the major pentatonic scale. Learn exactly where all the 3rds are, and practice bending them up a half step (the equivalent of one fret). On the next page is a simple lick that uses this idea.

Example 67

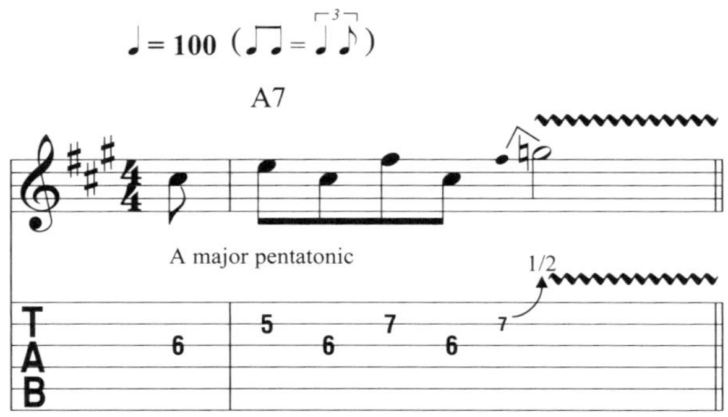

Now here's that same idea using the D and E major pentatonic scales:

Example 68

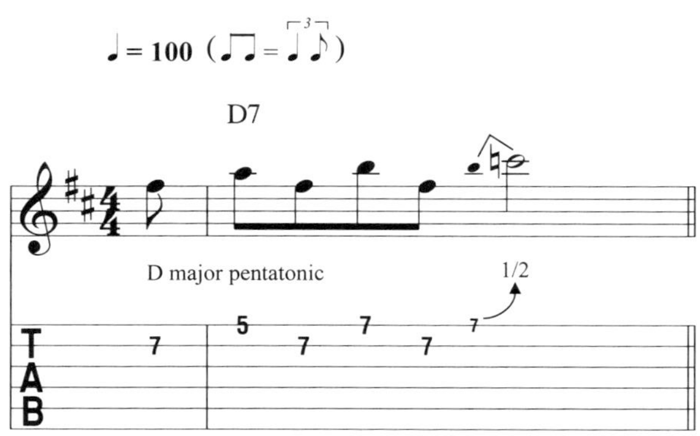

Example 69

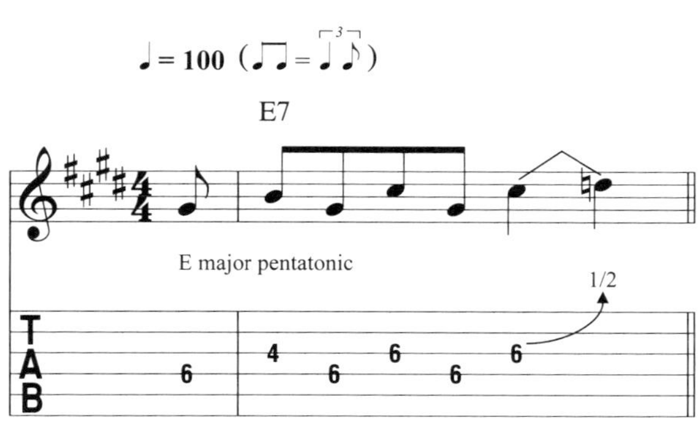

As you can see, we can transpose the same lick to fit each chord.

The Blues Scale

One essential scale we have not yet explored is the blues scale. Essentially, it is simply the minor pentatonic scale with the addition of one important note: the ♭5. I see it as a chromatic passing note between the 4th and the 5th. It can also add an interesting color as a stand-alone note (to the 1 chord, especially). Here are a few positions of the blues scale:

A Blues Scale

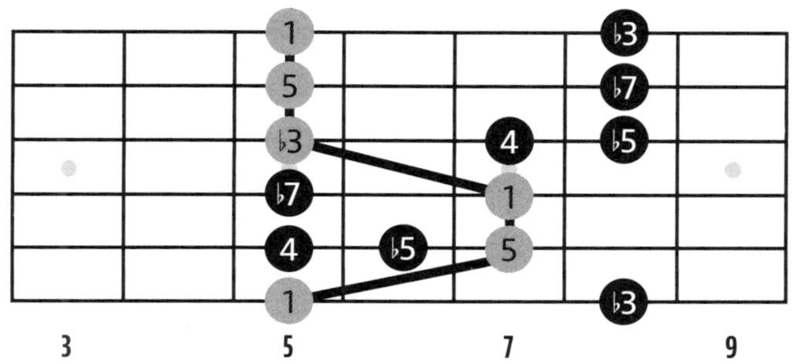

D Blues Scale

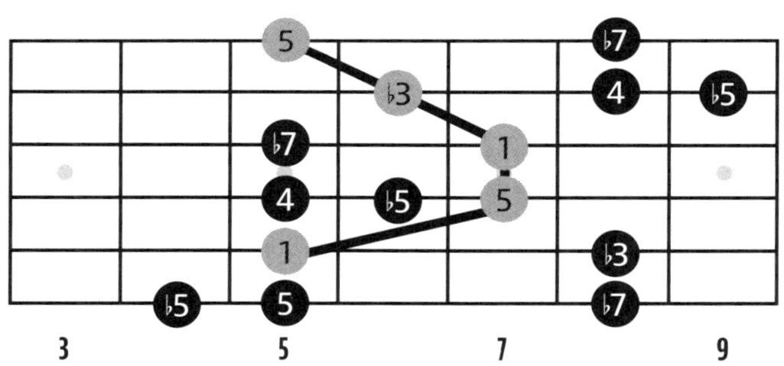

E Blues Scale

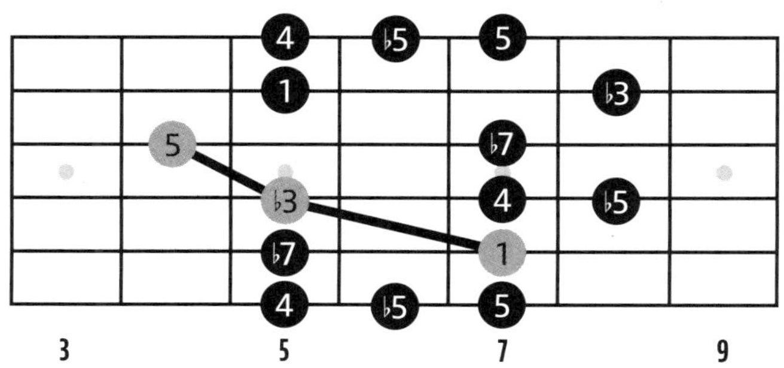

Now let's look at a solo that incorporates the use of major pentatonic, minor pentatonic, dominant pentatonic, and blues scales in addition to arpeggios:

Major and Minor

Example 70

Seven-Note Scales

Now that we've covered a bunch of pentatonic scales and arpeggios, let's move on to full seven-note scales. The most commonly used scale over dominant 7th chords is Mixolydian. This is the fifth mode of the major scale. We won't get too heavy into the theory of modes in this book, but for simplicity, think of it as a major scale with the 7th flattec (lowered by one fret). We already covered the Mixolydian scale when we learned about chord scales earlier in the book, but here are three scale positions for the chords of a blues in A:

A Mixolydian

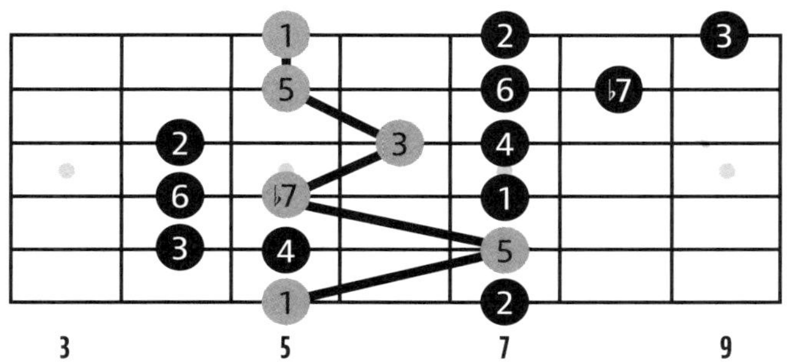

D Mixolydian

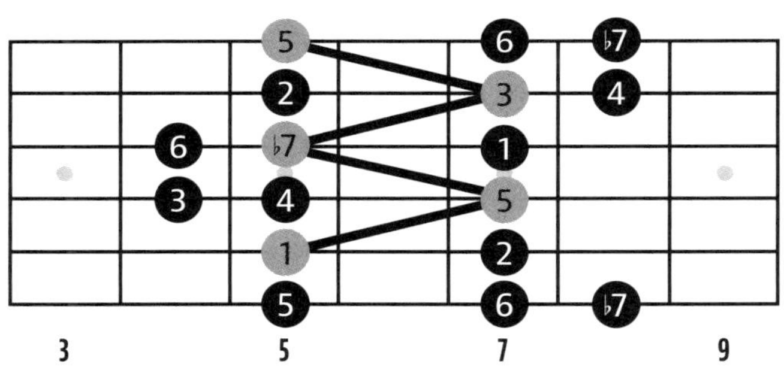

E Mixolydian

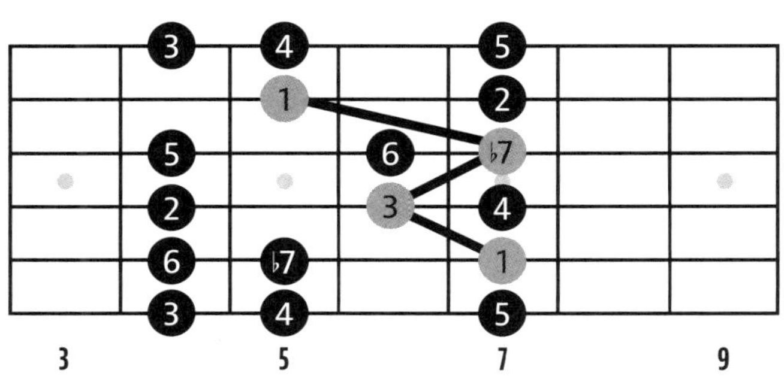

When soloing with a scale containing seven notes, we need to consider that most chords have four notes (a dominant 7th, for example). This means there are three notes in the scale that are less "at rest" than the others (the other notes match with the notes of the chord). Dominant 7th chords have the following intervals: 1–3–5–♭7. The Mixolydian scale has: 1–2–3–4–5–6–♭7. The 2nd, 4th, and 6th are the notes not shared with the chord. This doesn't mean we can't play them; it just means they sound less "at rest" than the other notes. You can see them as stepping stones, or a way to extend the quality of the chord with your soloing. For example, if we were to focus on the 2nd (which is the 9th over the octave), we would extend the sound of the dominant 7th chord to become a 9th chord. It's really good to know where the strong chord tones lie.

If you have learned your dominant 7th arpeggios from earlier in this book, you will see that these exist within the framework of the Mixolydian scale. Also, within this scale are the major pentatonic scales and dominant pentatonic scales. See if you can spot them inside the diagrams. You can see Mixolydian as being all of those notes layered on top of each other.

In order to have a strong sound in the blues as the chords change, I recommend you start on a chord tone of each new chord. The chord tone doesn't always have to be the root. Many people get into the habit of only starting a new scale from its root. For a strong sound, we can start on any of the chord tones (1, 3, 5, or ♭7), and it will give us a strong feeling of the chord changes underneath. Let's stick to starting on the 3rd for this example:

Example 71

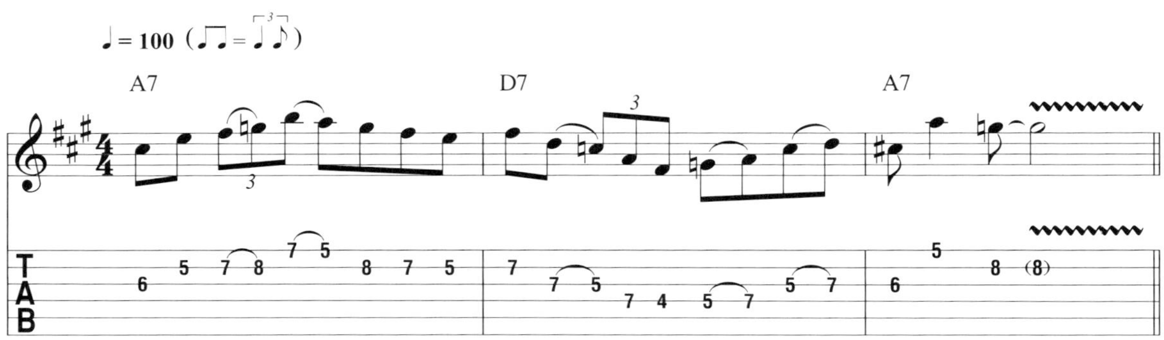

In this short, three-bar example, I wanted to demonstrate starting each new chord change from the 3rd of the relevant scale. Over the A7, we use A Mixolydian and start on the 3rd (C♯). On the D7, we use the D Mixolydian scale and start on the 3rd of that scale (F♯). Generally speaking, I like to vary my approach when soloing through a whole blues. Sometimes I might like to start on the 3rd, sometimes on the root, the 5th, the 7th, and so on. What is interesting is when we play the 3rd on the A7 (C♯), the ♭7 of the D7 is just a half step lower (C). These little micro-movements between chords often lead to a smoother connection and less disjointed feel. Simply starting from one interval on each chord can be a bit boring after a while, so feel free to experiment.

On the next page is a solo where I vary the starting note on each chord change and use various chord tones to start from (1, 3, 5, or ♭7). This time, I opted for a more modern, straight feel.

Modern Mixolydian Blues

Example 72

4 Exotic Scales and Tensions

Typically, when I am playing blues, I will use a combination of all the approaches we have covered so far. Rarely will I exclusively use any one approach. Nevertheless, it is important to really sink your teeth into all the information separately and gradually start to meld all the approaches into one.

Raising Scale Degrees

Continuing on the track of some unusual scales, I want to introduce the idea of raising the 4th degree in our Mixolydian scale. If you cast your mind back to the blues scale we covered earlier, you will remember that the blues scale adds a ♭5 interval. This gives a very distinct sound. If we raise the 4th in Mixolydian, it becomes a ♯4, which is the same interval as a ♭5. Let us explore this scale a little:

A Mixolydian ♯4

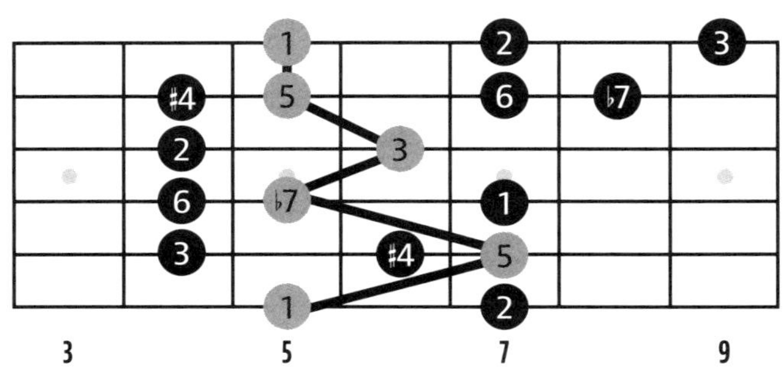

I tend to name this sale Mixolydian ♯4, but others often call it Lydian ♭7 or Lydian Dominant. It has a very familiar sound that you may recognize from the theme song of "The Simpsons." Let's take a look at this lick over A7 using A Mixolydian ♯4:

Example 73

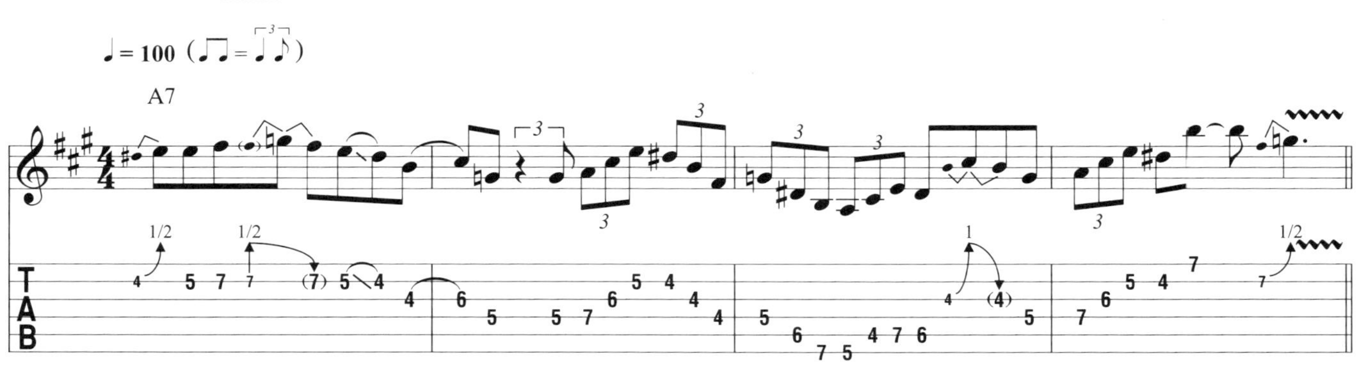

You may be starting to think that this sounds like jazz. Don't forget that jazz is an evolution of the blues, so there is definitely a link between the two. This is a more extreme version of the blues, but it still works just fine over a blues chord progression. If you mix in these elements with your more traditional blues licks, it will add a spice to your playing that will take the audience's ears by surprise.

We can also use the Mixolydian #4 scale on the IV chord of the blues, but we need to play D Mixolydian #4. As explained earlier, if we imagine the D7 being the I chord instead of A7, then that makes A7 the V of D7. Whenever we have a V chord, we can alter it to make the pull into the next chord feel stronger. This works especially well on the last two beats of bar 4 in a 12-bar blues. To illustrate this, let's look at the first six bars of the blues here:

Example 74

As you can see in bar 4, we spend two beats on the A7, and during the last two beats we alter the chord to have a #5 and introduce some tension pulling us more strongly into the next chord. There is also another way of looking at this. If we imagine a D9 chord up a half step, that is the same as A7#5 just with a D# bass instead of an A bass. (This is also known as a tritone substitution.) Both ways have the same effect:

Example 75

As we've already started learning the Mixolydian #4 scale, it's easier to view things the second way, as we can simply play D# Mixolydian #4 over the D#9 chord into D Mixolydian #4 over the D9 chord. It's worth mentioning that even if the backing track doesn't have the preemptive chord in measure 4, we can still play this melodically and imply it's there. Let's take a look at this in action with an expanded version of our previous lick:

Example 76

A much more simplistic approach would be to simply play a D#7 arpeggio over beats 3 and 4 of that fourth measure before it changes to the IV chord (D7) in bar 5. But these scales can add some excitement and give an exotic feel that listeners could be intrigued by. It's important to explore all of these options and use each one to taste. Each player is going to come up with something a little different, so I encourage you to explore. It is especially important to land on a strong chord tone when you arrive at your destination, which in this case is the IV (D9) chord. This same method also works playing into the iv chord of a minor blues, but in that case, the chord you're landing on would be minor. I made sure I landed on an F♯ over the D9, which is the 3rd of the chord. Here are the scale shapes I used for D and D♯ Mixolydian ♯4:

D♯ Mixolydian ♯4

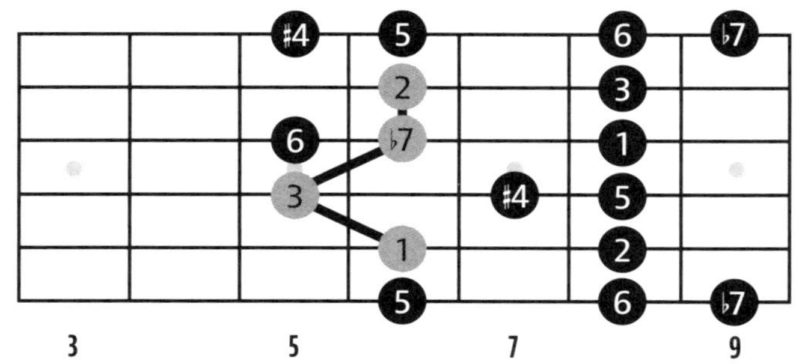

D Mixolydian ♯4

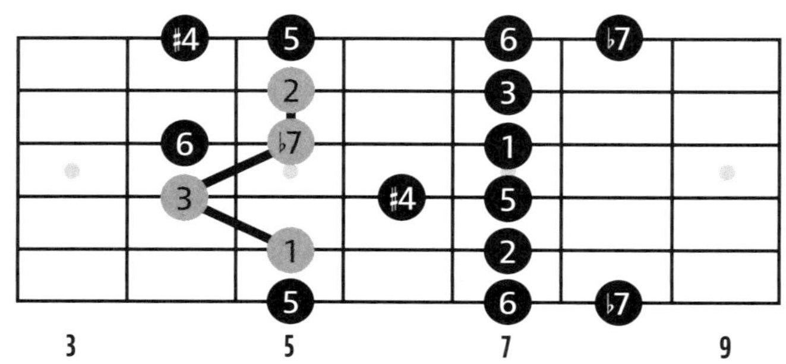

The other interesting thing to note is that on bars 9 and 10 of a 12-bar blues, we go from the V chord to the IV chord. This time, the V chord is not resolving to a I chord, so it will not be considered a functioning V chord. Therefore, we can add the kind of tension we did before. In fact, the D Mixolydian ♯4 works just well over both the E9 and D9 chords as that scale contains both chords. Below, I have highlighted both chords within the D Mixolydian ♯4 scale. Let's take a look:

D Mixolydian ♯4 over D9 and E9

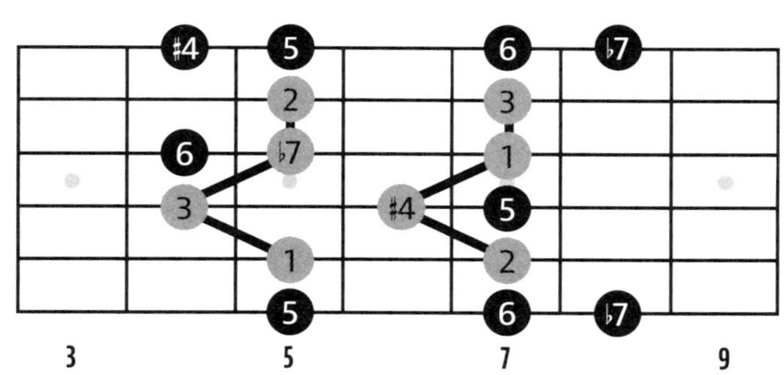

As you can see above, D Mixolydian ♯4 has the D9 and E9 chords within it. This is the reason it will work so well in measures 9 and 10 of the blues, as they're both in the same key (scale). When played over the E9, it technically becomes Mixolydian ♭6.

In measure 12 of a 12-bar blues, we get the V chord (E7 or E7♯9) returning back to the I chord in the first measure. This is a V–I resolution. We can therefore add tensions onto that V chord to make it pull back to the I chord more strongly. Just as we did in measure 4, we can simply play the Mixolydian ♯4 scale up a half step (one fret) from the I chord. This will work perfectly over the E7 or E7♯9 chord. It gives us a terrific tension that really seeks to be resolved. Let's add all this together to form an interesting solo:

Mixolydian ♯4 Solo

Example 77

Here is the A♯ Mixolydian ♯4, which is played over bar 12 of the previous solo:

A♯ Mixolydian ♯4

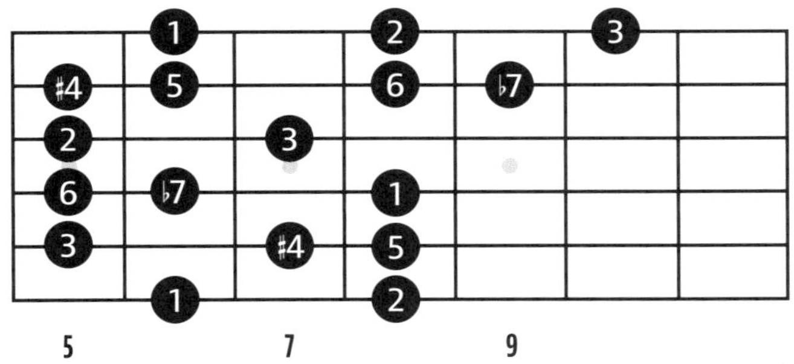

The Diminished Scale

Now that we have talked about some of the more "outside" and tense sounds, I want to briefly touch upon another cool option for adding tension to the music. This works in the same places we touched upon in the last example (e.g., bar 4 going in to bar 5 and bar 12 going back to bar 1). Instead of using the Mixolydian ♯4 a half step up from the destination chord, we will use the diminished scale a half step up from the chord it is coming from. For example, in bar 4 we have an A7 (I) going to D7 (IV). We can use the A♯ diminished scale on that 4th measure to resolve it to the D7. This causes our A7 to sound like an A7♭9 or A7♯9, which gives that stronger pull into the D7. Likewise, in bar 12 we can play an F diminished scale over the E7 chord to give a strong pull back to the A7 in bar 1. Let's take a look at the diminished scale:

A♯ Diminished Scale

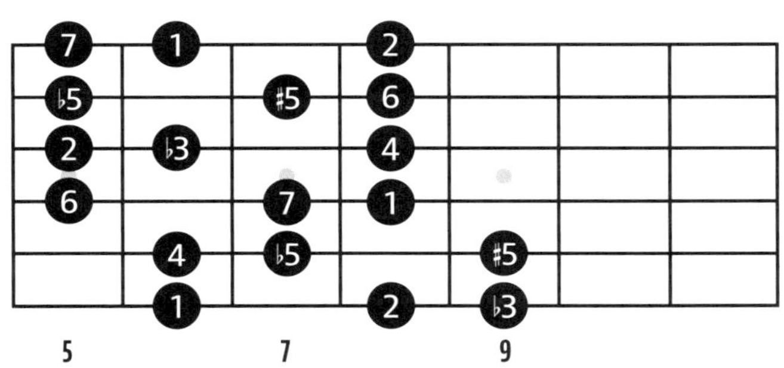

As you can see, this scale has eight notes instead of the usual seven notes we get in most scales. This is what we call a symmetrical scale, as it consists of a repeating pattern of whole steps and half steps. The intervals shown imply a B♭ root, but as we are superimposing this over an A7 chord, I will add A as the root so you can see the true intervals of this scale over the A7 chord:

A Half-Whole Diminished Scale

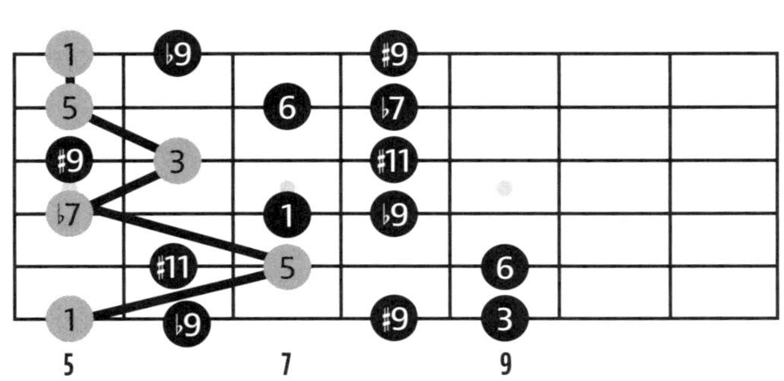

You can clearly see the A7 chord just by adding that lower A note. If we simply move this entire shape one fret higher, it will work over the E7 chord in bar 12. Let's take a look at a solo which implements this scale in the fourth and 12th bars:

Diminished Blues

Example 78

5 Triads and Triad Pairs

So far, we have mostly looked at scales, pentatonics, and four-note arpeggios. I also want to put some focus on triads, as I consider them to be one of the most important aspects of music for creating an interesting sound that still utilizes the notes from the scales, but in a less obvious way. If we consider that a triad is built with three notes and scales contain seven, we can see that triads are much sparser.

Exploring Triads

Let's explore how we can extract triads from any scale. Take the C major scale for example: C–D–E–F–G–A–B. If we use C as our starting note, the 3rd of C is E and the 3rd of E is G. Let's put those three notes together: C–E–G. This forms a C major triad.

Now let's build a triad from the D note in the C major scale: D–F–A. This makes a D minor triad, because D to F is one whole step and a half, and F to A is two whole steps. That means we have a formula of 1–♭3–5, making it a D minor chord. If we continue through the scale in the same manner, we get a total of seven triads, one built from each note of the scale. Here are the triads we end up with: C–Dm–Em–F–G–Am–B°.

Let's look at the last triad of B°. To form this, we took the notes of B, D, and F. Diminished triads have a formula of 1–♭3–♭5. To get from B to D, we go up a whole step and a half to get to the ♭3rd. Then, from D to F, we also go up a whole step and a half. Diminished triads are simply two of the same interval (♭3) stacked.

As you can see, we only get three types of triad out of a major scale: major, minor, and diminished. Be sure to memorize the order they appear in, as they will be this same order for any major key. The only thing that will change is that the new key will have different letter names. Any major scale will always yield the following chord types in this order: M–m–m–M–M–m–°. (Here I have used the following shorthand: Standalone letter M = major, m = minor, ° = diminished.) If we change the key to A major, we get: A–Bm–C♯m–D–E–F♯m–G♯°. And in the key of G we get: G–Am–Bm–C–D–Em–F♯°. Hopefully you get the idea.

Now let's take a look at the Mixolydian scale, which is the scale we will mostly be using to create our triads for the blues. As explained before, the Mixolydian scale is like the major scale but with the 7th flatted. Another way to see it is that it is in fact the major scale starting from the fifth degree (position in the scale). For example, the C major scale and G Mixolydian are the same scale starting from different notes. This is what we call a mode. The formula from Mixolydian starts from the 5, so it looks like this: M–m–°–M–m–m–M. It's the same order as the major scale, except it's starting in the middle of the formula (the fifth degree). Let's learn the A Mixolydian triads in 5th position on the fretboard:

Example 79

Here, we see the A Mixolydian scale harmonized as triads within one scale position. If you learned the scale position earlier in the book, it should already be familiar. It is simply the same notes arranged in a way that is less of a straight line walking up and down the scale. Playing with triads makes our playing sound more sophisticated and less scalar.

Pairing Triads Together

You may notice that the title of this chapter contains the words "triad pairs." A pair of triads can add up to six notes, assuming that neither of them share any of the same notes. To get the maximum amount of scale notes over two triads (6), the easiest way is to choose two triads that are next to each other. In the case of A Mixolydian, we could choose A and Bm as a pair. This would make A–C#–E from the A triad and B–D–F# from Bm. When you put those notes in a straight line, you get A–B–C#–D–E–F#. The only scale note we are missing is G. You can pick any triad pair, as long as they are within the harmonized scale. My favorite triad pair for use over an A7 chord is A and G. A has the notes of A–C#–E while G has the notes of G–B–D. In a straight line, that gives us A–B–C#–D–E–G (or 1–2–3–4–5–♭7). The only note missing is F#, which is the 6th. Let's look at the triad pair of A and G within our A Mixolydian scale shape. First, here is the scale shape we are using:

A Mixolydian

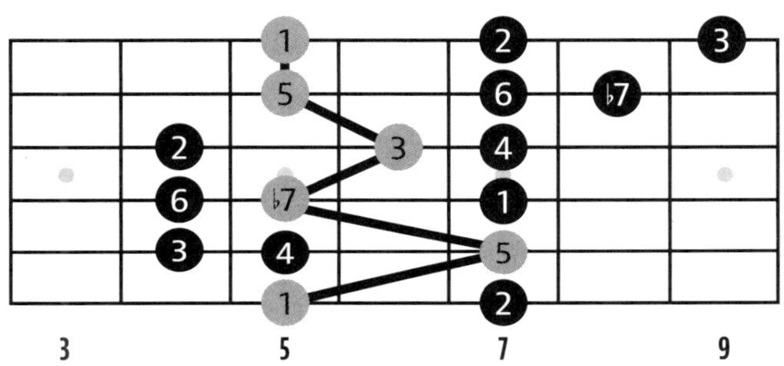

And here are our A and G triad pairs in every inversion within this scale position:

A and G Triads in A Mixolydian

Example 80

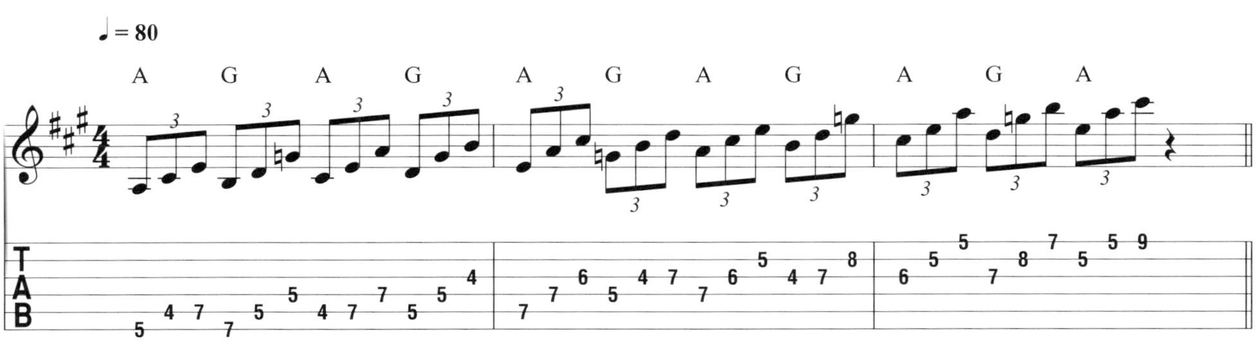

These create an interesting sound when played over our A7, A9, A7sus4, or A13 chords. When used creatively, these give us the flavor of Mixolydian without sounding like we're playing a scale. Next, let's look at the same thing for the D7 chord. For D7, we will use the same triad pair in relation to D Mixolydian. This gives us the triad pair of D and C, six notes of D Mixolydian. To keep this around the same fret region, we will use the following scale shape for D Mixolydian:

D Mixolydian

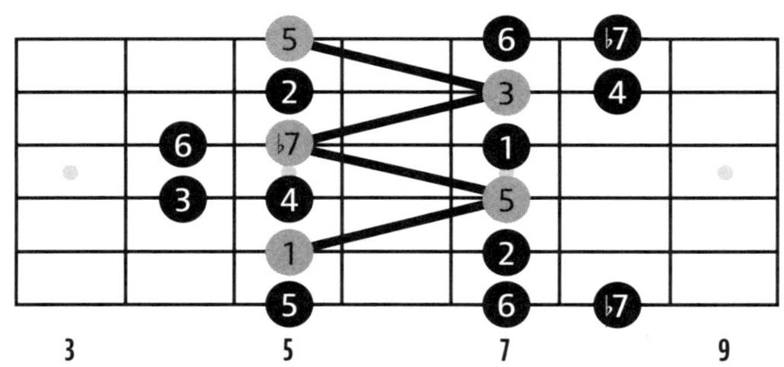

And here are the triad pairs of D and C contained within this scale shape:

D and C Triads in D Mixolydian

Example 81

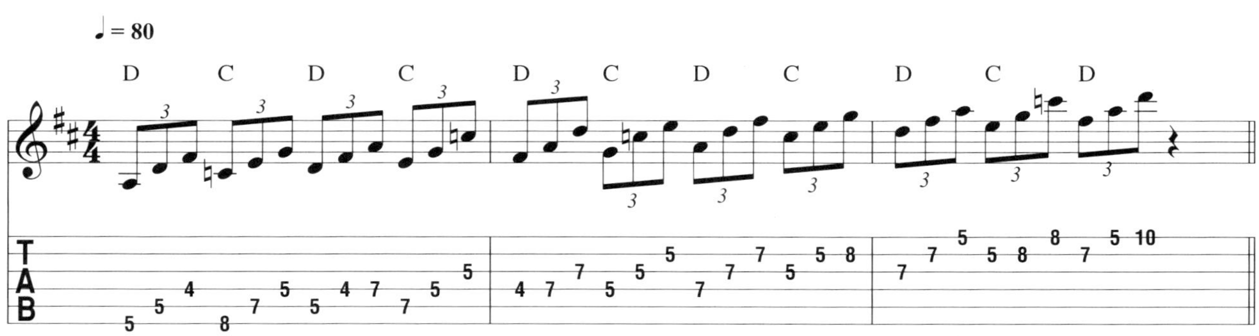

Be sure to get these under your fingers, and use fingerings that make it so you don't have to unnecessarily move your hand position. I will often use one finger and roll across when a note is on the same fret of an adjacent string, rather than using two fingers. Less is more!

Now let's talk about the E7 chord within the blues. We will draw our triad pairs from E Mixolydian, and use the triad pair of E and D. Hopefully, you start to the see the pattern. When playing over a dominant chord, we use a triad from the root (E) and a triad a whole step below that (D). This has been true throughout A7 (A and G), D7 (D and C) and E7 (E and D). Let's look at our scale position for E Mixolydian, located on the next page.

E Mixolydian

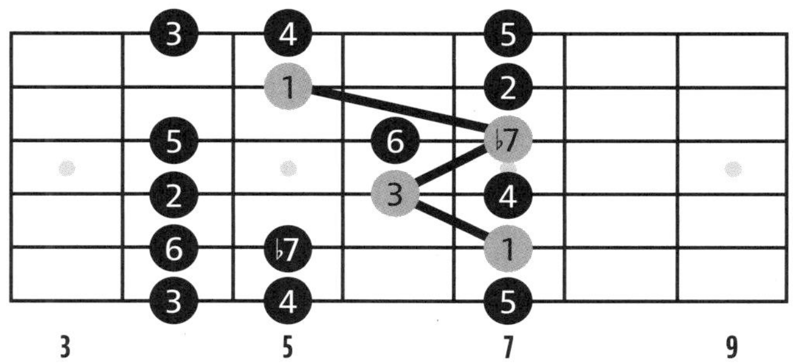

And now here are the triad pairs of E and D within E Mixolydian:

E and D Triads in E Mixolydian

Example 82

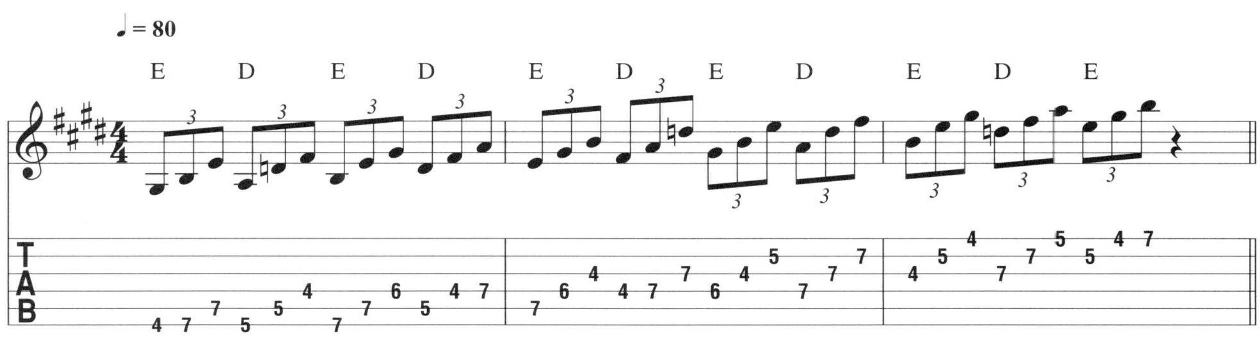

Now let's take a look at a solo that incorporates these triad pairs to outline the chord progression.

Example 83 appears on the next page to allow for easier reading.

Triad Pairs in the Blues

Example 83

The purpose of this solo is to reinforce outlining chord changes into your playing, but make sure you really know where these triads are coming from and study the scale shapes. In a solo, you might want to combine several concepts at once, rather than just sticking to one, but I recommend that you make these miniature studies a priority. Explore all of the triad options and really search within scale to find interesting things to play that will take the listener's ear by surprise.

6 Exploring the Fretboard

So far, we have mainly stuck to one area of the fretboard. Now I want to talk a bit about soloing in other parts of the fretboard, and ultimately seeing the fretboard as a whole. The most efficient way of learning the fretboard is to learn it in five chunks. This system is known as the CAGED system, and once these five chunks are put together, we end up covering the whole fretboard with whatever scale, arpeggio, pentatonic, or chord it is we're trying to learn. I am not going to go into a long-winded explanation on the CAGED system in this book, as there are many excellent books on this topic. I will lay out a few positions that we can play the blues in. Let's explore one of the ways below:

A Minor Pentatonic with Added ♭5 (Blues Scale)

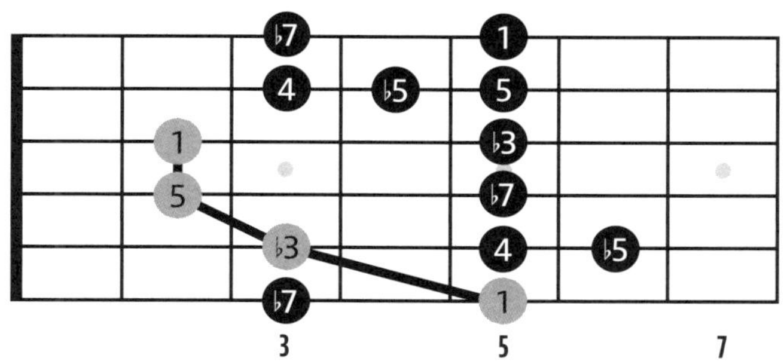

D Minor Pentatonic with Added ♭5 (Blues Scale)

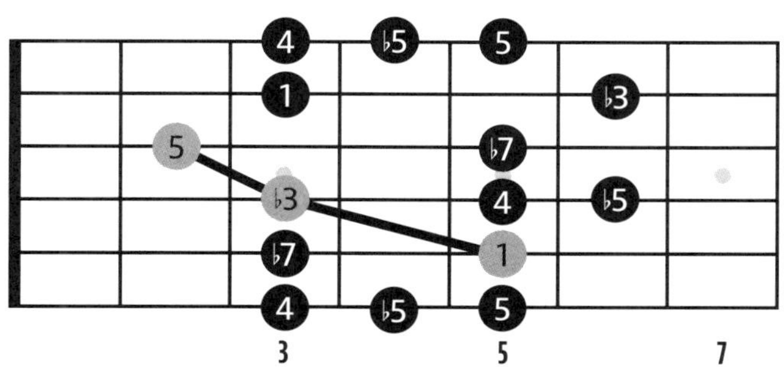

E Minor Pentatonic with Added ♭5 (Blues Scale)

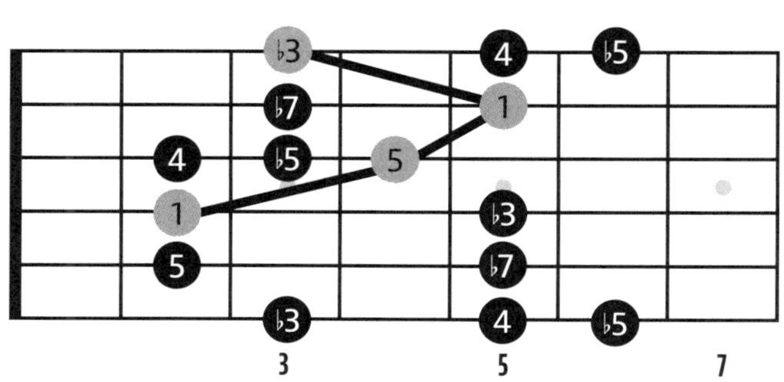

Here, we have the A minor pentatonic (or blues scale, if you add the ♭5) located around frets 2–5 for an A blues. Pay attention to where the root notes are in each, as they are not the lowest note in the scale. Also pay attention to the notes which are connected with a line. These form the minor chord associated with each of the minor pentatonic scales. To practice playing these, I recommend that you start and end on the lowest root to first learn where each scale is measured from. This helps us when we want to change keys with the new shapes. For example, here is how I would first practice the E blues scale, starting and ending on its root:

Example 84

It is so important that we fully understand all the notes we are playing, especially where the root is located. Otherwise, it makes it very difficult when we want to change to another key. Right now, the root of E is located on the second fret of the D string. If we wanted this scale to be played as G blues, we would need to situate the root on fret 5 of the D string, as that is a G. To play this scale position as A blues, we would situate the root on the seventh fret of the D string. If you aren't that familiar with where notes are on the D string, then that would be something for you to study first. I recommend you practice moving these shapes around the fretboard and playing them in as many different keys as possible.

Here are various major pentatonic scales in the same fret region:

A Major Pentatonic

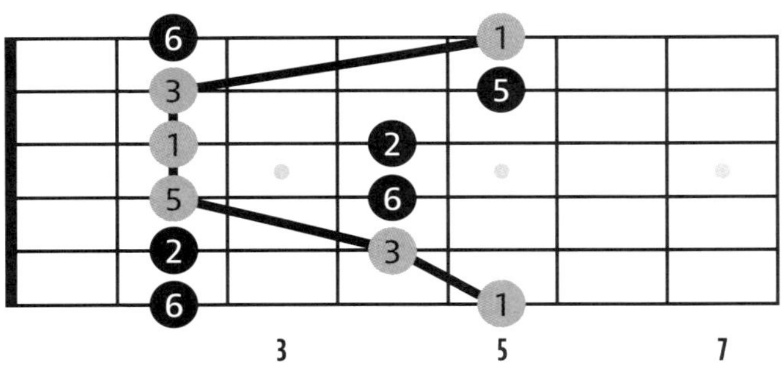

D Major Pentatonic

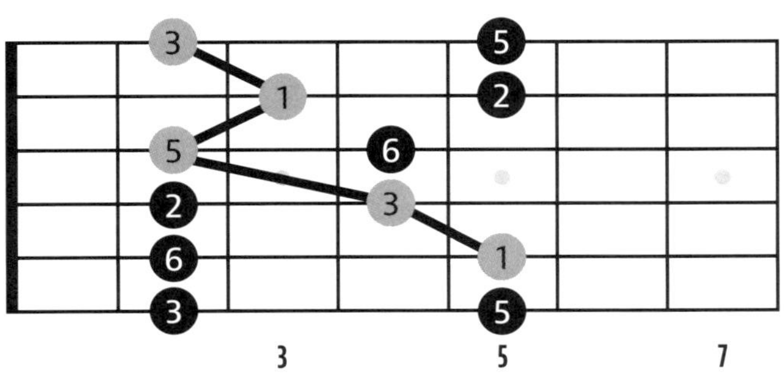

E Major Pentatonic

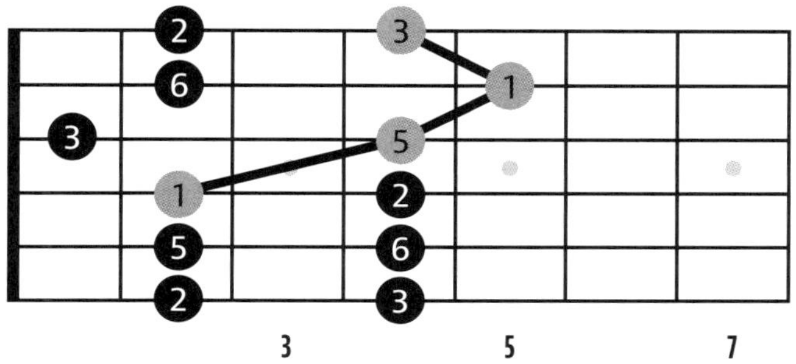

Using all the shapes we have learned so far (five shapes of each scale and repeating the C shape), we can play in any key, anywhere on the neck. Take the time to learn each shape, and move them to every other key (there are 12 keys in western music). This will help you learn to play anything you want.

Now let's look at the dominant 7th arpeggios in this part of the neck:

A7 Arpeggio

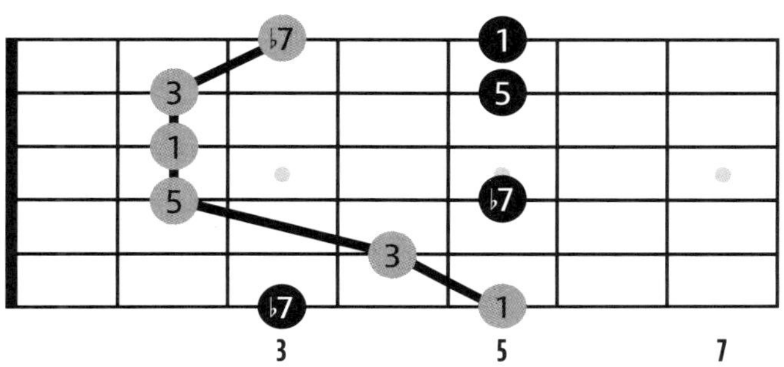

D7 Arpeggio

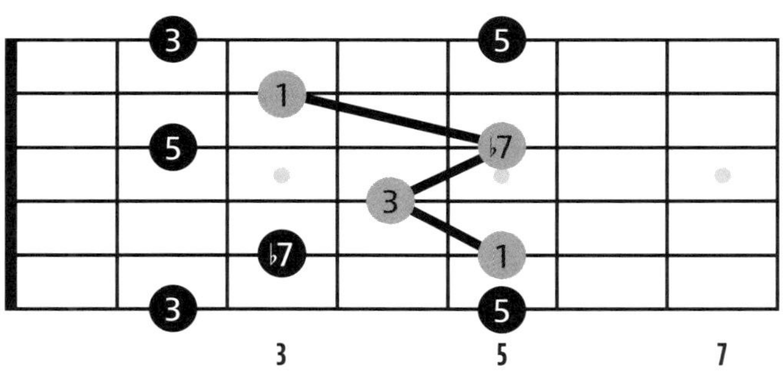

E7 Arpeggio

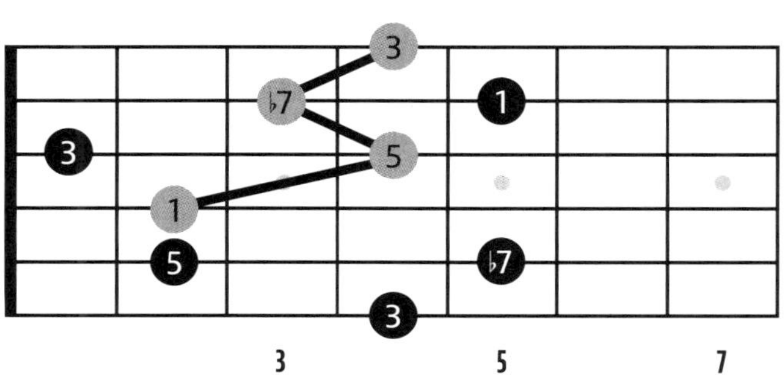

Learning these shapes on different parts of the neck seems like a lot of work, but they will really open things up for you to be equally fluent in all areas of the fretboard with no blind spots.

Here are various dominant pentatonic scales in the lower positions:

A Dominant Pentatonic

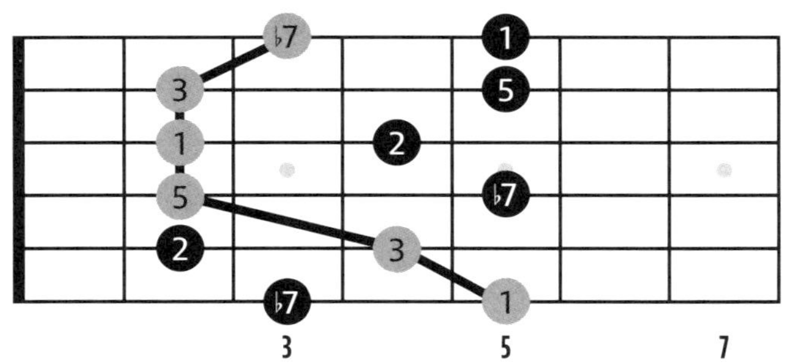

D Dominant Pentatonic

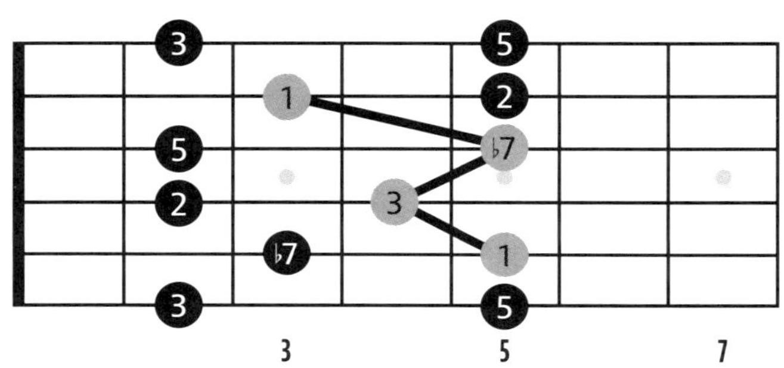

E Dominant Pentatonic

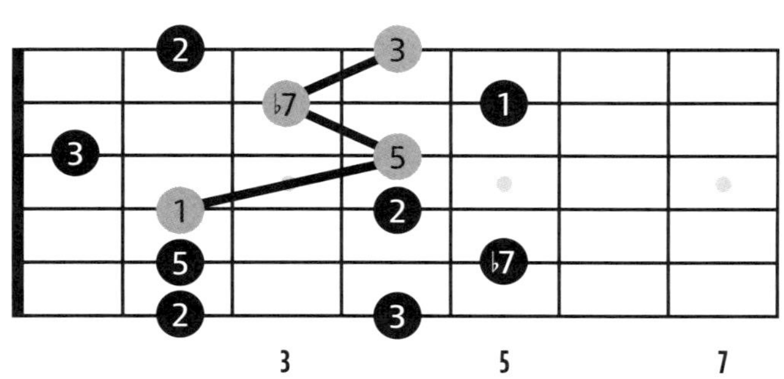

Finally, here is the Mixolydian scale in this fret region:

A Mixolydian

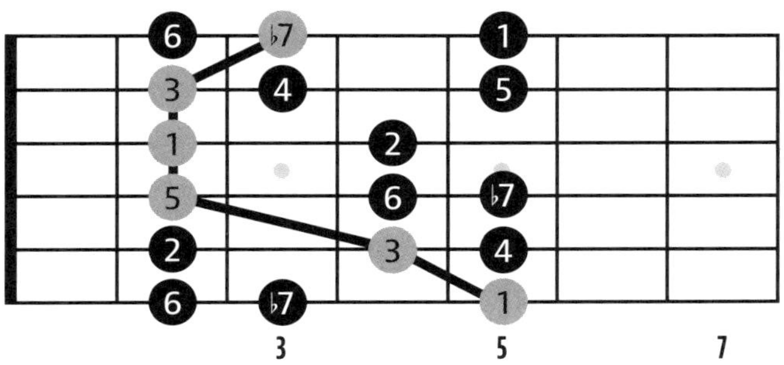

D Mixolydian

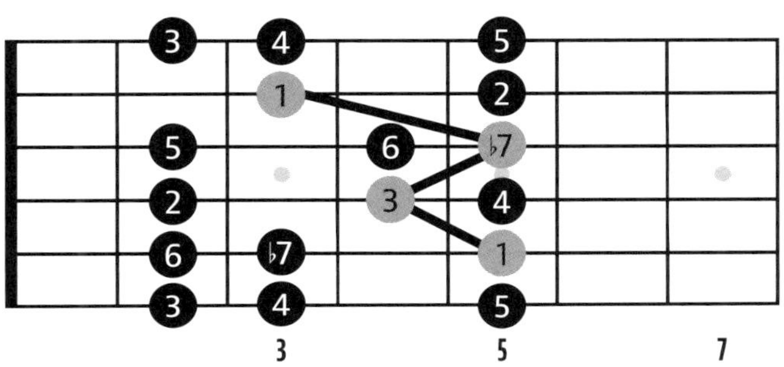

E Mixolydian

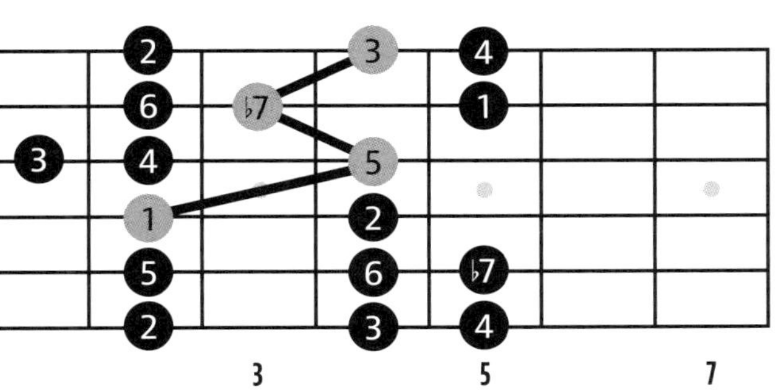

With all this information, let's look at a solo in A on the next page that covers this lower part of the fretboard. It covers minor pentatonic, major pentatonic, and dominant pentatonic scales.

Venturing Outside

Example 85

With this solo, you can see the application of these positions and how the fretboard can open up into new territory. You may find that these new positions feel uncomfortable at first. This is perfectly normal, as most players spend all their time soloing in one position, so it's not surprising that moving outside of that will feel awkward. Stick with it, and you will start to see results. This chapter is intended to introduce you to other positions, but I encourage you to explore other areas of the neck also.

7 Soloing over Extended Blues Progressions

This chapter explores the soloing approach over the more advanced blues progressions we talked about at the beginning of the book. The first progression I want to solo over is an eight-bar, slow 12/8 blues progression, which is as follows:

Example 86

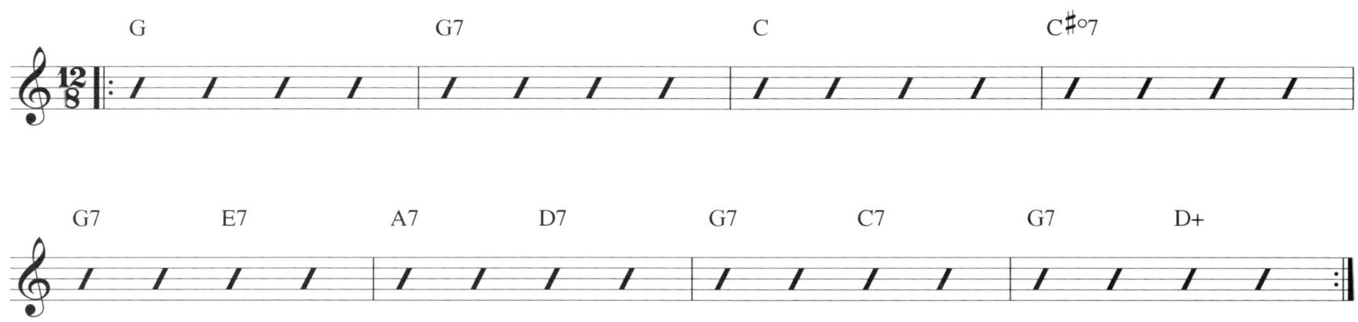

This is a good example of a situation where the blues isn't necessarily always 12 bars. There are some interesting moments where we see chords that are not in our traditional 12-bar blues progression. For example, we see a C♯°7 which consists of the following intervals: 1–♭3–♭5–♭♭7. The ♭♭7 interval could also be seen as a 6th, but it continues the symmetrical nature of the chord, which is to stack minor 3rds on top of one another. We also have the VI7 chord (E7) and II7 chord (A7), which we have not had to solo over as yet. Finally, in bar 16, we see the D augmented chord (D+), which consists of the following intervals: 1–3–♯5. That is simply a stack of major 3rds, which is symmetrical in nature like the diminished 7th chord, which consists of a stack of minor 3rds. Let's learn the diminished and augmented arpeggios, as we haven't covered those yet. I have also highlighted the chord shapes with a connecting line:

C♯°7 Arpeggio

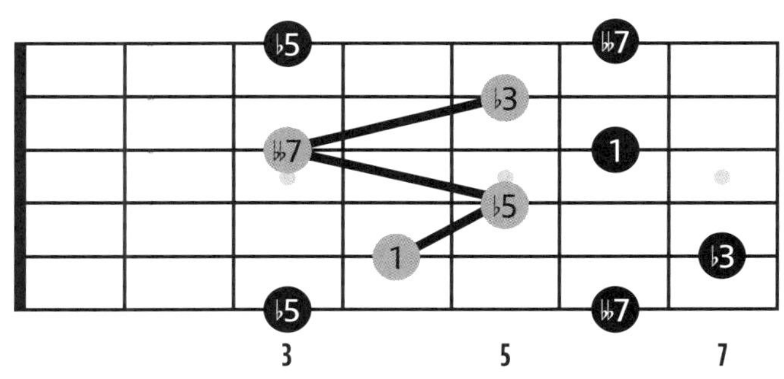

D+ Arpeggio

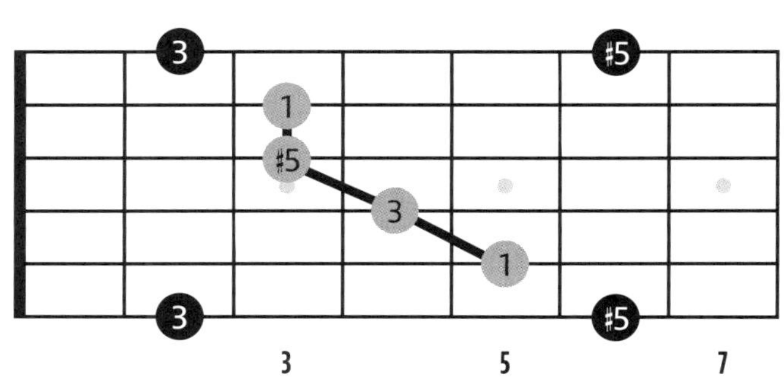

It's also worth mentioning that D+ can be treated as any V chord which is resolving to I, and simply play Mixolydian ♯4 up a half step from the I chord (A♭ Mixolydian ♯4). This works perfectly over the D7 chord. Take the time to practice and memorize these arpeggios, as they will help us to make sense of the solos we learn. We can also simply play the C♯ diminished scale instead of the arpeggio, but the arpeggio really gets to the heart of the chord. With the VI7 and II7, we can simply play around the arpeggio, the minor pentatonic, the dominant pentatonic, or even the Mixolydian, but in this context I would be hesitant to go for the Mixolydian because of the context of the chords. Another choice is to consider the VI7 to be the V of the II7 chord, and therefore play the Mixolydian ♯4 a half step up from the II7 chord (B♭ Mixolydian ♯4). The same rings true with viewing the II7 as the V of the V (D7). These are all options, but perhaps not the bluesiest of options. It's good to experiment and decide for yourself. I will mainly stick to chord tones in the following solo. Let's dive in and look at a solo over this progression:

Hitting the Changes

Example 87

Now let's talk through each measure of this exercise. In measure 1, we started out with the G7 arpeggio with the ♭3 added, which could also be seen as the G minor pentatonic with the major 3rd added. The last few notes in that measure, we borrowed two notes from G Mixolydian, the ♭7, the 9th, and finished on the root. Measure 2 used the same kind of approach, and this time, we finished on the 9th. In measure 3, we played over a C chord, and this bar mostly used a combination of C Mixolydian and chord tones for C7. In measure 4, we incorporated our new C♯ diminished arpeggio to great effect. Measure 5 saw us starting out using our G minor pentatonic and adding the major 3rd. In the second half of this bar, we switched to an E7 chord and reacted by soloing using the E7 arpeggio and E minor pentatonic. Those shapes are as follows:

E7 Arpeggio

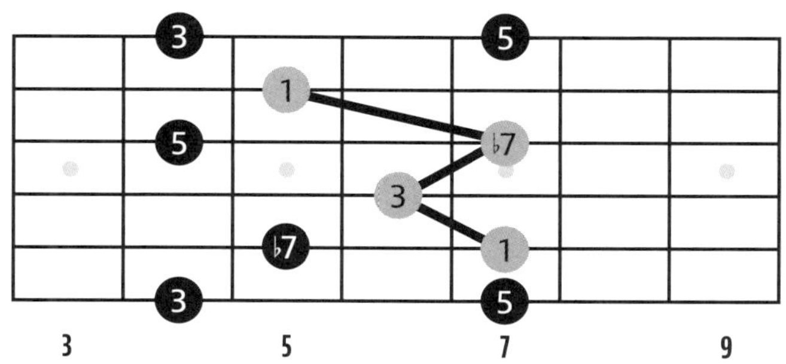

E Minor Pentatonic

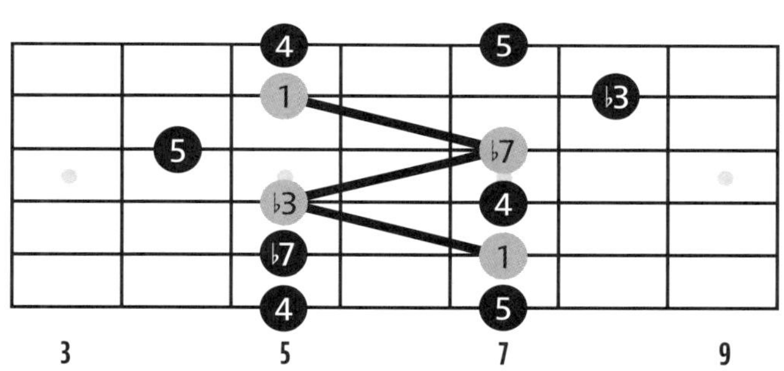

In the first half measure 6, we see the use of the A7/A minor pentatonic combination using the same shapes we had over G7, albeit one fret higher. Then, the chord changes to D7 and we see the use of the D7 arpeggio integrating some chromatic notes. Here is the shape we used to play D7:

D7 Arpeggio

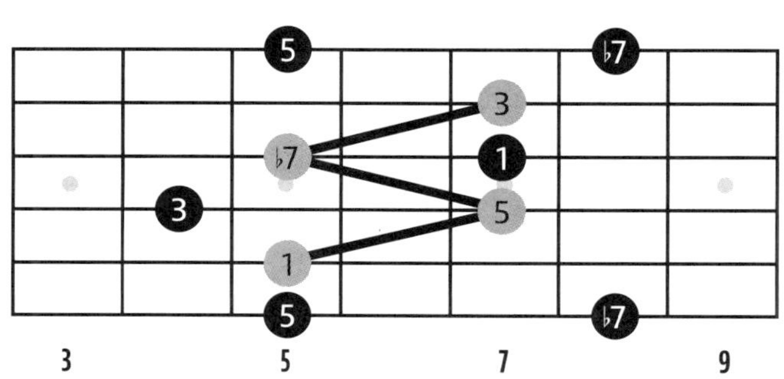

In measure 7, we see the use of the G7 arpeggio in the first half and C7 in the second half. Both times we use the minor 3rd as a passing note to lead into the major 3rd. Finally, in measure 8, we see the use of the G minor pentatonic/G7 arpeggio in the first half, and then we chromatically lead into the D+ arpeggio. We used the D minor pentatonic for the last couple of notes, being sure to bend up the minor 3rd to a major 3rd to fit correctly with the D augmented chord, which contains a major 3rd.

Now let's look at an even more advanced jazz/blues. This progression has a lot of twists and turns, and presents some new ideas for us within a simple, 12-bar structure. This blues is in G and has the following chord progression:

Example 88

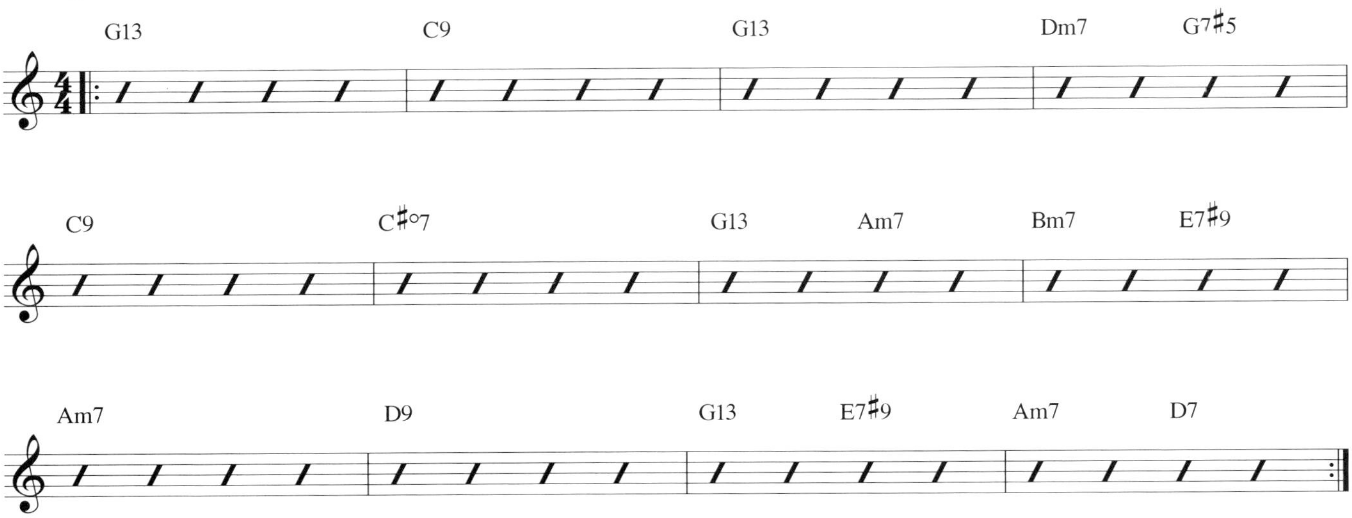

This progression is one of the most complex we can get, but it still retains the feel of a blues and can still be approached as such. I want us to explore a solo over this progression that really nails all of the chord changes. I will include a combination of approaches throughout. Let's take a look:

Advanced Blues

Example 89

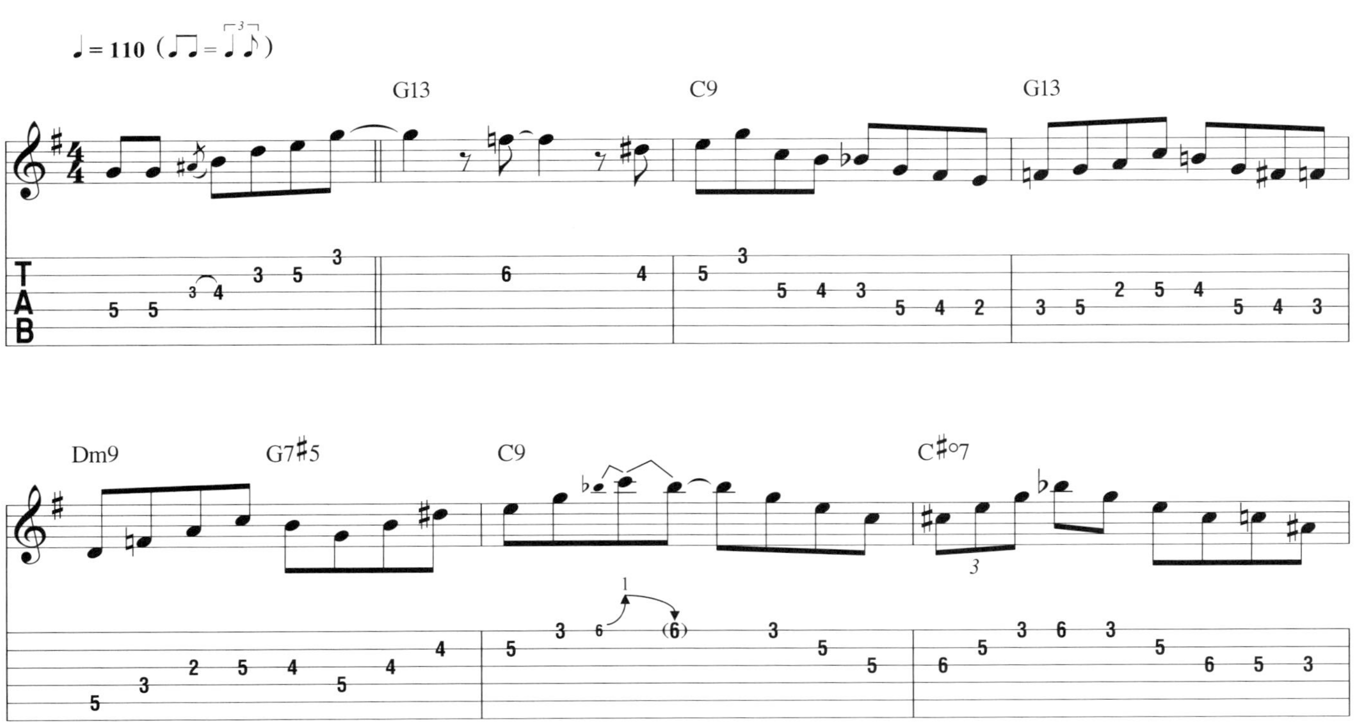

The first measure is a pick-up bar, which uses the G major pentatonic, hammering from the ♭3 to the major 3rd for a bluesy effect. In the next measure, we land on the ♭7 (F) of the G13 chord. Then, we play a note chromatically below the major 3rd of the C9 chord. While technically a wrong note, it preempts and leads the listener's ear nicely into the C9 chord. In the next measure, we play over the C9 using some chromatic passing notes and the ♯4 of C Mixolydian ♯4 scale. We use the G Mixolydian scale over measure 4 with a chromatic descent between the root and ♭7 for the last three eighth notes. In measure 5, we play a Dm7 arpeggio over the Dm7, and we play the root, 3rd, and ♯5th over the G7♯5, which really just outlines that chord. In measure 6, we play around the C7 arpeggio and use a bend in order to move from the ♭7 to the root of the chord.

In the next measure, we play over the C♯°7 using the C♯°7 arpeggio and lead downwards with the diminished scale for the last three notes. In measure 8, we play our G Mixolydian ♯4 over the first half of the bar and then play the Am7 arpeggio adding in the 9th (B) over the Am7. In measure 9, we use the same arpeggio we used over the Am7 but two frets higher. Over the E7♯9, we borrow from the B♭ Mixolydian ♯4. Measure 10 sees the use of an Am9 arpeggio. In measure 11, we make use of the D7 arpeggio with a ♭3 chromatic lead-in to the major 3rd. Measure 12 see the use of some more chromaticism with a preemptive chromatic lead-in to the E note over the E7♯9 chord, which we play over using the B♭ Mixolydian ♯4. The final measure sees a simple Am7 arpeggio over the Am7 and then a D augmented arpeggio over the D7 chord to add the ♯5 tension on the D7, as it is the V chord to G13 at the top of the blues.

8 Minor Blues

For a final solo, I would like us to look at the minor blues. From a soloing perspective, we can simply play the blues scale, and this will suffice. But I want us to explore other options to make the minor blues a little more interesting. Here is the minor blues progression we will be soloing over:

Example 90

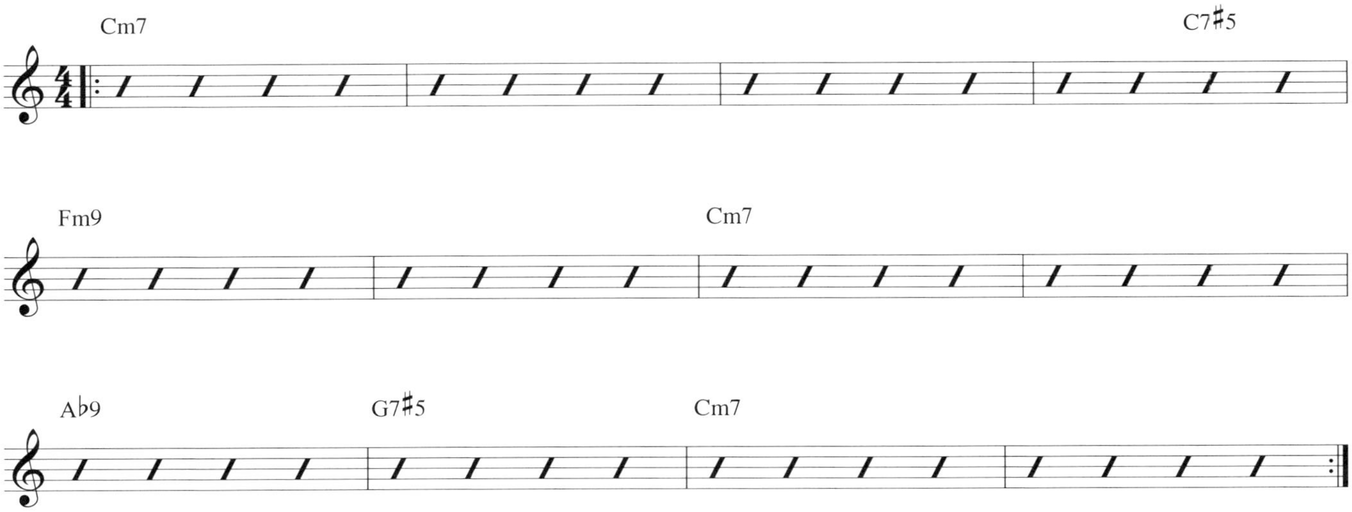

As well as approaching the minor 7th chords with minor 7th arpeggios, I want to explore the idea of playing a major 7th arpeggio from the minor 3rd of the chord. This gives us a very nice, minor 9 extended sound. For example, here are the intervals of an E♭maj7 arpeggio when compared to a C root (played over a Cm7 chord). The root is not played, but it is highlighted in red for reference:

E♭maj7 Arpeggio Compared to C Root

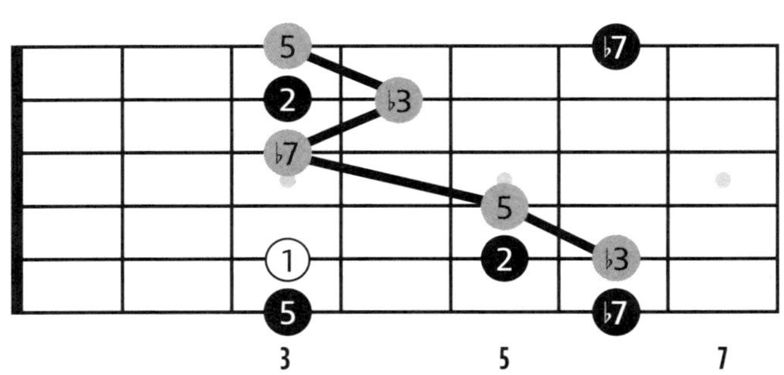

As you can see, the E♭ note itself becomes the minor 3rd compared to the Cm7 chord we are playing it over, and we also end up with the 5th, minor 7th, and 9th intervals, which gives us an extended sound when played over the C minor 7th chord. Similarly, we can also use an A♭ major 7th arpeggio (also a minor 3rd up from the minor chord) over the Fm9, and this will give us the same effect.

A♭maj7 Arpeggio Compared to F Root

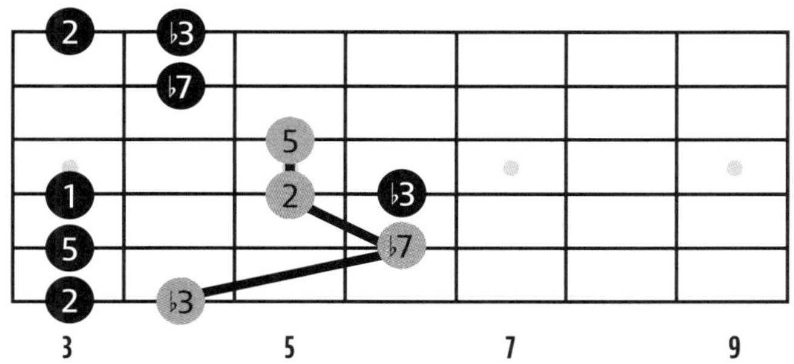

Another scale we can use over minor chords in a minor blues is the Dorian scale. Let's take a quick look at C Dorian for the C minor:

C Dorian

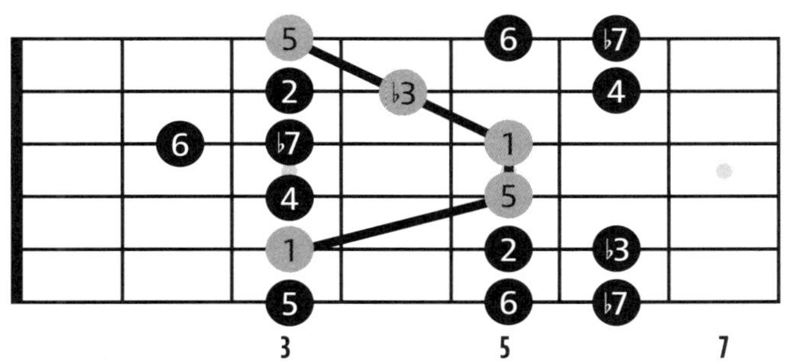

I have highlighted a familiar C minor shape with the connecting lines (an Am shape transposed) to give context when transposing this shape.

Here is F Dorian for the Fm9 chord:

F Dorian

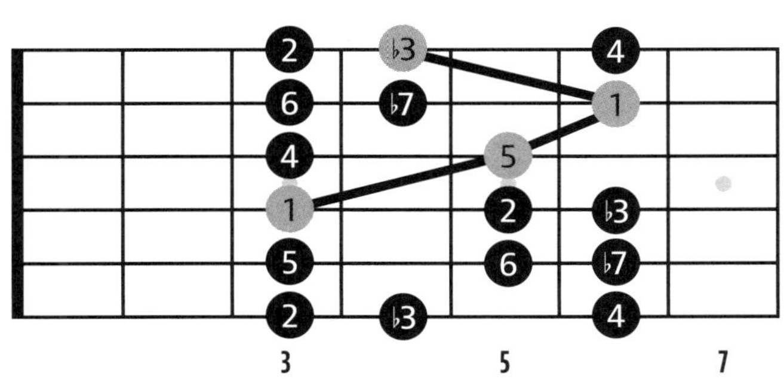

I highlighted an F minor chord with the connecting lines for context.

Let's take a look at a solo over this chord progression (it appears on the next page).

Minor Blues

Example 91

There are some chromatic notes added for a cool effect, but the minor 7th and minor 9th chords are mostly using the major 7th arpeggios a minor 3rd up from the root as mentioned earlier. Also, some notes from Dorian and the blues scale were used. On the C7♯5, we see this as a V chord resolving to Fm9, which acts as the i chord to the C7♯5. We used F♯ Mixolydian ♯4 over the C7♯5 (use Mixolydian ♯4 a half step up from the i chord is the rule here).

Over the A♭9, this is a non-functioning dominant chord which does not need to resolve, so we use the A♭ Mixolydian ♯4 scale over this one. Finally, over the G7♯9, we treat this as a V chord using the Mixolydian ♯4 a half step up from the root of the i chord which is Cm7, so we use D♭ Mixolydian ♯4 here.

Conclusion

I hope you have gained a lot of insight and information from this book. It really was a labor of love that I hope you will enjoy for many years to come. Some of the best advice I ever had was from Frank Gambale, who said, “Take your time, there is no rush.” These are such simple yet true words. Don’t feel the need to get all of this information crammed in at once. This information can be absorbed over months or even years, so take your time and have fun applying some of these concepts into your playing.

It was my intention to aim this book at players looking for more interesting lines to play in a blues context, all while keeping the same basic blues foundation intact. It is my belief that all modern electric guitar players should have a foundation of blues in their playing, as most modern electric styles have their roots in the blues. After all, the blues is the heart and soul of the notes. Although I cover some fairly advanced practically-applied theoretical concepts, I want you to keep in mind that feel and timing are always number one, above all else. Try not to lose sight of that as you play through these exercises. I also want you to understand that you can still apply some of the more intricate concepts and still maintain a solid blues feel throughout. Think about this book as a way of expanding your existing blues vocabulary. Above all else, experiment and have fun. That’s what music should be: fun!

Enjoy, and see you around!

Nick Kellie

About the Author

Award-winning guitarist, educator, columnist, and, now, author Nick Kellie has been actively teaching and performing since 1994. Boasting a resume that includes working with noted virtuoso Frank Gambale and various hit pop groups, Nick has released recordings under Steve Vai’s Digital Nations label to much acclaim in addition to performing in some of the world’s most iconic venues. Currently, he teaches at the leading contemporary music schools in Los Angeles, California, and he regularly contributes to other online and print publications such as *Jamplay.com* and *Guitar Player* magazine.

MASTER THE Blues

BLUES GUITAR Instruction Books from Hal Leonard

All books include notes & tablature

12-Bar Blues
by Dave Rubin
The term "12-bar blues" has become synonymous with blues music and is the basis for other forms of popular music. This book is devoted to providing guitarists with all the technical tools necessary for playing 12-bar blues with authority. Covers: boogie, shuffle, swing, riff, and jazzy blues progressions; Chicago, minor, slow, bebop, and other blues styles; soloing, intros, turnarounds, and more.
00695187 Book/Online Audio..............$19.99

75 Blues Turnarounds
by Michael DoCampo with Toby Wine
This book/audio pack teaches 75 turnarounds over common chord progressions in a variety of styles, including those of blues guitar greats like Albert King, Johnny Winter, Mike Bloomfield, Duane Allman, Jeff Beck, T-Bone Walker and others.
02501043 Book/Online Audio..............$12.99

100 Blues Lessons
Guitar Lesson Goldmine
by John Heussenstamm and Chad Johnson
A huge variety of blues guitar styles and techniques are covered, including: turnarounds, hammer-ons and pull-offs, slides, the blues scale, 12-bar blues, double stops, muting techniques, hybrid picking, fingerstyle blues, and much more!
00696452 Book/Online Audio..............$24.99

101 Must-Know Blues Licks
by Wolf Marshall
Now you can add authentic blues feel and flavor to your playing! Here are 101 definitive licks – plus a demonstration CD – from every major blues guitar style, neatly organized into easy-to-use categories. They're all here, including Delta blues, jump blues, country blues, Memphis blues, Texas blues, West Coast blues, Chicago blues, and British blues.
00695318 Book/Online Audio................$1.99

Beginning Blues Guitar
by Dave Rubin
From B.B. King and Buddy Guy to Eric Clapton and Stevie Ray Vaughan, blues guitar is a constant in American popular music. This book teaches the concepts and techniques fostered by legendary blues guitar players: 12-bar blues; major & minor pentatonic scales; the blues scale; string bending; licks; double-stops; intros and turnarounds; and more.
00695916 Book/Online Audio..............$12.99

Beginning Fingerstyle Blues Guitar
by Arnie Berle & Mark Galbo
A step-by-step method for learning this rich and powerful style. Takes you from the fundamentals of fingerpicking to five authentic blues tunes. Includes graded exercises, illustrated tips, plus standard notation and tablature.
14003799 Book/CD Pack....................$22.99

Brave New Blues Guitar
by Greg Koch
A kaleidoscopic reinterpretation of 16 blues rock titans is the hallmark of this Greg Koch book with over three hours of online video lessons. It breaks down the styles, techniques, and licks of guitarists including Albert Collins, B.B. King, Eric Clapton, Jimi Hendrix, Stevie Ray Vaughan, Johnny Winter and more.
00201987 Book/Online Video.............$22.99

Chicago Blues Rhythm Guitar
by Bob Margolin & Dave Rubin
This definitive instructional guitar book features loads of rhythm guitar playing examples to learn and practice, covering a variety of styles, techniques, tips, historical anecdotes, and much more. To top it off, every playing example in the book is performed on the accompanying DVD by Bob Margolin himself!
00121575 Book/DVD Pack.................$22.99

Everything About Playing the Blues
by Wilbur Savidge
An ideal reference guide to playing the blues for all guitarists. Full instruction on blues theory, chords, rhythm, scales, advanced solo technique, beginnings and endings, riff construction and more. Includes play-along audio with 12 jam tracks.
14010625 Book/Online Audio...............$29.99

Fretboard Roadmaps – Blues Guitar
by Fred Sokolow
Fretboard patterns are roadmaps that all great blues guitarists know and use. This book teaches how to: play lead and rhythm anywhere on the fretboard; play a variety of lead guitar styles; play chords and progressions anywhere on the fretboard, in any key; expand chord vocabulary; learn to think musically, the way the pros do.
00695350 Book/Online Audio..............$15.99

Hal Leonard Blues Guitar Method
by Greg Koch
Real blues songs are used to teach the basics of rhythm and lead blues guitar in the style of B.B. King, Buddy Guy, Eric Clapton, and many others. Lessons include: 12-bar blues; chords, scales and licks; vibrato and string bending; riffs, turnarounds, and boogie patterns; and more!
00697326 Book/Online Audio..............$19.99

How to Play Blues-Fusion Guitar
by Joe Charupakorn
Study the scales, chords, and arpeggios most commonly used in the blues-fusion style and how to use them in this book. You'll also examine how artists like Matt Schofield, Mike Stern, Scott Henderson, and John Scofield put their own spin on the blues/fusion format.
00137813 Book/Online Audio..............$19.99

Blues You Can Use Series
by John Ganapes

Blues You Can Use
This comprehensive source for learning blues guitar is designed to develop both your lead and rhythm playing. Blues styles covered include Texas, Delta, R&B, early rock & roll, gospel and blues/rock.
00142420 Book/Online Media...........................$22.99

More Blues You Can Use
This follow up edition covers: pentatonic scales, single-note tremolo, double-string bends, reverse bends, shuffle rhythms, 6th and 9th chords, boogie patterns, chord substitutions, vibrato techniques, and more!
00695165 Book/Online Audio.........................$22.99

Blues Guitar Chords You Can Use
A reference guide to blues, R&B, jazz, and rock rhythm guitar, with hundreds of voicings, chord theory construction, chord progressions and exercises and much more.
00695082...$17.99

Blues Licks You Can Use
Contains music and performance notes for 75 hot lead phrases, covering styles including up-tempo and slow blues, jazz-blues, shuffle blues, swing blues and more!
00695386 Book/Online Audio..........................$17.99

Blues Rhythms You Can Use
Develop your rhythm playing chops with 21 progressive lessons: basic rhythm theory; major and minor blues; 8th, 16th and triplets; extensions; passing chords; lead-rhythm style; funky blues; jump blues; blues rock; and more.
00696038 Book/Online Audio..........................$22.99

HAL•LEONARD®

Order these and more publications from your favorite music retailer at halleonard.com

1020
312